MOUNTAIN FOLKS

Of Old Smoky

Veta Wilson King

Copyright 1997 by Veta Wilson King
Mountain Folks Publishing
2907 Jones Cove Road
Sevierville, TN 37876

All the stories in this book, except 'Memoirs of Living in Big Greenbrier', were written by the author. Most appeared originally in *The Mountain Press* Newspaper. They are slightly edited for book use and are reprinted by permission of *The Mountain Press*.

ISBN 0-9662017-0-1

Library of Congress
Catalog Card Number
97-92864

Printed in the United States of America
By The Mountain Press, Sevierville, Tennessee
Cover design by LaPrees Advertising and Design.

Eagles Cove Photography

Donnie, Veta, Tyler & Allison

Mountain Folks is dedicated to my late great uncle, Wiley Ogle, brother, Jim Wilson, nieces and nephews: Anita, Amy, Gina, Melanie, Lori, Rachel, Matt, Kendra, Mark, Kellie, Andrew, Katie Jo, Justin, Alex, Jennifer, Tracy, Jessica, Jason, Andrew, and Sharon.

It is most especially dedicated to my husband, Donnie, our two children, Tyler and Allison, Dad, and to the memory of Mama.

Acknowledgments

Special thanks to Aunt Kate Beck, Mrs. Lucinda Ogle, Mr. Herbert Clabo, and Mrs. Beulah Linn, Sevier County Historian, for their kind assistance. I am grateful to Mr. Gene Aiken for permission to include a portion of the photos that appeared in his *Mountain Ways* books.

On The Cover

Front cover: David and Rintha Watson with children, Dicie Ellen, Ruth Ann, and Richard Henry. Photo taken approximately 1906.

Back cover: Jim and Josie Ownby with daughter Cecil. Photo taken approximately 1903.

Great Smoky Mountains photograph by Darrell Wilson.

"Every good gift and every perfect gift is from above,
and cometh down from the Father..." James 1:17

"As we have therefore opportunity,
let us do good unto all men... Galations 6:10

Leather Britches

The smell of chimney smoke begins to fill the air as the sunlight brightens the brilliant red, orange, and yellow fall colors. A small farmhouse, the homeplace of Luther and Minnie Proffitt Rolen, sits in a community known as Chucky or Jerry's Fork — not a close neighbor in sight. The time is in the 1930s.

As the cool nights set in, it is time to put another of mother's hand made, warm, soft quilts on the bed.

On the back porch hang shab beans or leather britches, and sage and red peppers that will later be used in making pork sausage. In the fields there are stands of corn tops that look like small Indian tee pees and bundles of fodder drying in the sun so the Rolens will have winter feed for the cows. Corn stalks stand tall and bare with only roasting ears left to dry for chicken, cow, and hog feed and for taking to the mill to be ground.

Soon, shelling corn will add a few more calluses to the hands of the Rolen children. Corn cobs will make great ammunition for corn cob fights or for the Rolens to use with chicken feathers — just to watch them twirl and drop to the ground.

Dark greens cover part of the garden ground, and sweet potatoes are dug and wrapped individually in newspaper to be stored in the attic. Fat pumpkins ripen in the field, and it is time to pick enough cotton for another winter quilt or two.

Just before frost, the Rolens, Anna Lee, Erma Dee, Auburn, Gene, and their parents are busy pickling late beans to be placed in the spring house and holing up cabbage, turnips, and potatoes. They work hard not to lose any fall harvest as they place these foods in a hole in the ground and cover them with straw, dirt, and planks — enough to keep out the hard mountain winter freezes. Apples are picked and dried or sulfured.

There must be fun in the work of threshing clay peas. The dried peas are placed in a tow sack (a sack made from yarn spun from coarse tow fibers.) The Rolens beat the peas with a stick to separate them from the hulls. The dried peas settle to the bottom of the sack, and the hulls are raked off the top.

Leaves crackle underfoot as the Rolens walk back into the woods to cut firewood with a crosscut saw or gather chestnuts and chinkapins.

1

The round chinkapins (of the chestnut family) are threaded on a string and worn the same as beads around children's necks. The Rolens and their neighbors wear them to school to snack on during the day.

Children are outside most all fall days in the Chucky community (later to be known as a part of Jones Cove.) They are hulling walnuts and cracking them to sell the kernels and selling chestnuts to the peddler, Ben McMahan, who comes by with his horse and wagon. They sell them at Dave (Beaner) Webb's country store.

If there's any time left after gathering the fall harvest, the Rolen children enjoy the crisp, cool weather in play. They squirrel hunt with flips (sling shots) made from innertube rubber and forked dogwood limbs. They play whoopie hide (hide and seek), running base, and marbles. At Halloween, there's more fun in being a spook out after dark with other children than in trick-or-treating. The Rolens throw a sheet over their heads and go to two or three neighboring houses where they are given apples for treats.

As the community folks harvest their crops, the church members at Bradley's Chapel, New Salem, and Howard's View talk in revivals of a spiritual harvest. Just as there's an urgency for gathering crops as they ripen, preachers preach about this spiritual harvest indicating the urgent need for workers to spread the gospel. The Rolens walk to all three fall church revivals, sometimes two weeks in length. The walk to the night services is lighted only by moonlight. The ground below the children's bare feet begins to be chilly as they reach the more distant church services... services that are so good, the Rolens could stay on and on.

School days are interrupted by revival meetings, and there are days when children must leave early to work at gathering crops. There are field days at the county fair just before fall, and the basketball team walks to neighboring schools for games.

Back at home in the kitchen, there's the smell of apple butter cooking over a wood cook stove. Minnie Rolen stands steadily stirring the pot in an all day chore as she makes a delicious sweet for morning biscuits. Fall days are filled with the smell of something good in the kitchen as the Rolens make gooseberry butter and jelly, pumpkin stack pies and just everyday cornbread.

In the evenings, the Rolens sit around the fireplace and talk or read. The room is dimly lit by coal oil lamps and firelight. The fireplace serves as a place where neighbors gather for visits and a place for cooking in cast iron pots or baking bread on the hearth. It keeps out the winter cold, and it provides solace for a mother and her sick child in the middle of the night.

Gene, Anna Lee, and Erma Dee sit today on the porch of the old white frame house. They talk of those early years in Jones Cove as the evening sun shines out across the porch. Life was filled with the hard work of families who struggled to keep food on the table, but life was less complicated, the Rolens say. Neighbors were quick to have a roofing to put a new barn roof on or quick to take up a crop when someone was sick. Even though many daylight hours and early morning hours were occupied in work, people took time to be friendly, to visit, and do a kind deed.

When families began buying automobiles, Gene Rolen remembers that you could lie in your bed at night and know by the sounds of the motor who was driving by. Slowly, more and more changes came to Jones Cove through electricity, television, better jobs, better roads, more money, and more independence. While the Rolens may not wish for living through the seasons exactly as when they were children, they do wish for the way of life when neighbors had time for long visits and children had not a care in the world.

Luther and Minnie Rolen
in the Chucky Community, 1918

Courting

"He looked at me and kind of grinned, and I looked at him and kind of grinned, then he walked me home from church," said Lela Reagan Teaster as she told about the beginning of a courtship that led to her marriage to Bruce Teaster.

Teaster and her two sisters-in-law shared memories about their young dating or 'courting' years at Elkmont and nearby in the 1930s, and '40s, and just after they moved from the Great Smokies.

She said she and her future husband spent time walking or talking on the front porch swing or in the chimney corner. He told her, "I'm going to join the CC's if you'll marry me," then went to work out some money. "Dad gave me two dollars for two cane bottom, straight chairs," said Teaster. Some of their first belongings included the two chairs, an oil lamp on the wall, a home made mattress, and they bought two plates and two bowls. Lela Reagan Teaster had equal employment opportunity, even in her day. She pulled one end of an old cross cut saw and her husband the other as they cut wood for a community school.

Iva Teaster Whaley slyly grinned, and gave the idea that not all couples waited until after marriage to do their kissing in her courting days. She remembered young people dating in numbers. "Joe Parton would take a truck load to Gatlinburg to the movies," Whaley said. And, a bunch of young people would walk around on Sunday evenings. "The Trail of the Lonesome Pines," at the Tennessee Theater was the saddest picture Whaley ever saw in her life. She cried all through the movie on this triple date (two of the three were blind dates.) She laughed as she thought how mismatched the blind dates were.

She remembered she had to sit on her date's lap; he was a good bit smaller than she. "I told him, I'd feel better if you'd sit on my lap," she said.

Whaley later married Hansel (Hank) Whaley in 1938. He had operated an apple orchard business at Fighting Creek near Elkmont.

Myrtle Cogdill Teaster, then 16, was in her sister's kitchen, barefoot, scrubbing the floor when Woodrow Teaster arrived before daylight to get married. Earlier, he had proposed under a pine tree above Wonderland Hotel as the two stood sheltered from a spring shower. He had asked her parent's permission three times before, but her mother, Molly, would not allow it because she was so young. Molly Cogdill told her to wait one year, then she could have permission if she still wished to marry Woodrow.

Myrtle Teaster's father intervened; he told Woodrow, 'Molly, her mommy won't ever give up for you to marry her.' So, he sent the couple on to Sevierville to the Court House to wed, saying to call if they needed him. Woodrow had sent by Bruce Trentham to Knoxville and purchased a wedding ring for two dollars. The two drove away from Elkmont with Myrtle Teaster hiding in the car as she passed her mother's house. They went to Sevierville, probably to Carr's Dry Goods, where Teaster bought his new bride a pretty new dress, blue with a big white collar, and a new shirt for himself.

The Teasters were married; they took along Woodrow Teaster's cousin to sign for Myrtle Teaster's father. The groom forgot to pay the Judge. He continued to laugh over the years saying because he didn't pay, they were not legally married. The couple began their married life at Bear Wallow, above Elkmont, at Woodrow's parents. After a few days staying with Woodrow's sister and her husband, the Teasters soon found that Myrtle's mother held no grudges for their actions.

Earlier, Woodrow sent his brother-in-law, Perry Ownby, down to the Cogdill's to borrow a bread pan because he wasn't quite ready to face his new mother-in-law. It was on the Saturday they moved into their new home across from Lem Ownby's at Jake's Creek. All along, Molly Cogdill had been sending dish towels and asking for the two to come home.

Myrtle's husband's first job, as a newlywed, was working for 'Old Man Cochran' for 25 cents a day from daylight to dark delivering milk up and down through Club Town and assisting in his orchard.

As with many mountain couples in those days, these three couples started with few belongings and worked hard to provide a better life for their families. Their fun young courting years started them on a journey of happiness through many years and many children and grandchildren.

*Myrtle Cogdill and Woodrow Teaster
during their courting days in about 1931*

*Lela Reagan and Bruce Teaster
courting at Happy Holler around 1940*

Mountain Ingenuity

A little ingenuity went a long way in the deep woods of the Great Smokies before modern times.

When Coy Ogle was only a boy, he put some of that mountain ingenuity to work so he could play. His parents, Levi Evans Ogle (named for Preacher Richard Evans) and Nancy King Ogle, were leaving for a visit when he saw the Johnson kids coming through the field. Young Coy's parents had told him to stay home and keep the geese out of the garden. "I can't watch the geese and play, too," thought the boy, so he cut some small sticks and propped their beaks open. The geese could not eat the garden... and he could play. It must have been a strange sight when Ogle's parents arrived home early to find all the geese with their beaks wide open.

Henry McCoy (Coy) Ogle would, in later years, use that ingenuity to put together a prosperous farm on Big Dudley in the Great Smoky Mountains. He was born in 1878 in a family of two boys and five girls. The family had moved to Big Dudley from Two Mile Branch at the Sugarlands to plant an apple orchard. Coy and his brother Ashley Ogle farmed, and their sisters attended Mossy Creek Teacher's College in Jefferson City (now Carson Newman) or Murphy College in Sevierville.

Coy Ogle married a community girl, one of his classmates, around 1900 - Laurinda Proffitt Ogle.

Iva Wright, Coy Ogle's daughter, and Glenn Cantrell, his grandson, remember and talk about the Ogle home place at Dudley.

They talk of the orchard that produced hundreds of bushels of apples in the fall and required a two story apple barn for storage. Wright recalls using an apple gatherer made of canvas material with four ropes at each corner and a hole in the middle. There was a person holding each rope while one, usually Wright's brother Lloyd, climbed the apple tree and shook the fruit onto the canvas. The apples fell down and rolled to the hole in the center then dropped into a bushel basket underneath. The gatherer prevented most of the fruit from bruising. Once the apples were off the trees they were graded to be taken to market in Knoxville. Those that did not make the grade were made into cider for the family using a hand-cranked cider mill.

Taking the apples to market was a greater opportunity for Ogle than just selling his orchard produce. By the time this horse trader had been to Knoxville and back, he had sometimes traded his wagon team two or three times.

Marketing was also an opportunity for a young girl to make ties with someone far from these mountains. Cantrell's mother Sarah Veatress Ogle wrote her name and address on one of the eggs that was traded to the community store. Some time later she received a letter from a girl in New York who had purchased the egg. The two became pen pals for a while after that.

Cantrell's "Pappy" (Grandpa) got an early start at building up his farm. He raised a lot of cattle, and in the spring he drove them farther back in the mountains to graze. Once the cows were in place, Ogle cut trees down over the mouth of the holler leading out of the grazing area so the cows could not wander back. Other than checking on the cattle from time to time, Ogle had little to do with them. Still, by fall, they were so fat they could hardly walk home, Cantrell was told.

Ogle, using even more ingenuity, planted his own chestnut grove even though the Great Smokies were full of them. The chestnuts were taken to market.

The Ogle farm was made up of a blacksmith shop, a portable saw mill that was brought in twice, a stationery cane mill for making molasses, a corn grinding mill on Dudley creek, and the orchard. Coy Ogle had about fifteen stands or hives of bees for mountain honey and pollination of the orchard.

Cantrell remembers his "Pappy" as a good manager. Over time he had purchased about seven smaller farms and had tenant farmers living on them. By 1922, Ogle had bought his father's farm in the Glades which he primarily used for hay fields. He moved to a farm-house on Ogle Road so his daughters could be near Smoky Mountain Academy to attend high school. After going back and forth to Dudley to continue farming, it wasn't long before Ogle sold out to the National Park and lived the remainder of his life in the Glades.

By the time Coy Ogle reached his nineties, this lean mountain man's head full of dark hair had turned snow white. His last days in the Glades were spent in his rocking chair telling his grandchildren stories of his youth. He continued to be full of wit with a desire to win a good family debate.

And he puttered about the farm, not too old to set out just one more young apple tree.

Coy Ogle and Grace, his daughter

Trunk Treasures

Old family trunks were full of historic treasures in these Great Smoky Mountains. Items were carefully passed down through generations that gave glimpses of another time.

Great Great Grandma Celia (Celie) Proffitt Ownby had stored in a family trunk an old deed for one of the early land purchases in this area.

The hand written deed, dated April 3, 1828, was for Indian land, according to family history told to Glenn Cantrell, a descendant of the Proffitts. It read, "To Benegah (or Benejah) Proffitt and others I Do Hereby Give a Plot of land Border(ing) on Waters of Dudley Creek 5000 akres or somewhat for l. team oxen. l cart l long rifel, l Powder Pouch Bullet mols (molds) 3 Bag corn 6 Hen 2 roster. l kettel l oven 2 Cow 3 Hog. other considerasuns to have this Day onwards Witnes Middelton Whaley J Baley McMahan" (signed with an 'X') and an Indian symbol by Gatr (or Gata) Bird.

Family members wonder if the trade may have been made because the Cherokee nation was being removed from the Great Smokies to the west due to the Indian Removal Act in 1830.

The Proffitt family lived in the Jones Cove area and did not move to Dudley Creek until several years later. The next record that Cantrell has, is a copy of a January, 1863 will by Jackson Proffitt (the son or grandson of Benagah Proffitt). In this, he willed the Jones Cove homestead farm of six hundred acres, more or less, and the five thousand acres, more or less, on the waters of Little Dudley to his wife during 'her natural life or marriage,' then to his six sons in equal parts. To his four daughters, Proffitt bequeathed each to have one horse worth one hundred and fifty dollars.

Jackson Proffitt then entered the War Between the States where he died in service. Jackson's son Jim or James (married to Martha - Middleton Whaley's granddaughter) may have been the first of the Proffitts to settle at Dudley Creek, said Cantrell.

The acreage in the Proffitt family holdings included land from near Glades Road to the top of Round Top (now known as Mt. Winnesoka), said Cantrell. James and his family settled a few hundred yards from the present day Gatlinburg-Pittman High School entrance on Highway 321.

Much of Dudley Creek was vacated around the 1930's when the National Park purchased private farms. By this time several new families had already purchased pieces of the original 5,000 acres; yet portions of the Proffitt family's purchase from Bird remain in the Proffitt family today.

An early hand-drawn map, (drawn around the teens or twenties) by one Dudley Creek resident shows a few corn grinding mills along the creek and a blacksmith shop. There was a store where mail was left for folks farther out and a ball field at 'Hump' field. Dr. Fish was one Dudley Creek resident, and there was a Primitive Baptist Church at Little Dudley and a Baptist church and school building near the ridge that separated and served both Little and Big Dudley.

More than a hundred and fifty years have passed since this transfer of land between Native American ancestors and their white neighbors. Through historic documents such as these found in trunks the bridge between then and now, somehow, seems shortened.

The Happiest Girl

A handmade afghan drapes the wooden rocker where 'Granny' (Viola Clabo) Henry sits by her Warm Morning wood and coal burning heater. Years of warming cold winters have burned the once shiny dark heater to a rough brown. Granny, age 90 in 1993, laughs easily as she recalls earlier years of child raising - before arthritis and when her eye sight was far better. Her granddaughter's woolly gray cat gets cozy in a chair by the fire as 'Granny' talks.

Her hair is as black today as in her childhood. It could be, she guesses, because she descended from a great grandmother who was 'full blooded Cherokee Indian.'

As a little girl, 'Granny' Henry lived at Caney Creek, south of Pigeon Forge, off the Parkway. "You ought to call this Caney Creek, because there's a little (sorghum) cane patch in about every flat bottom up through here," a man once told folks there.

At seventeen, Viola Clabo married Simeon Henry, from the Jay Ell community. In two years, her first son, Earl, was born. As a child, Granny, the same as many in her day, thought the midwife or 'granny woman' brought new babies. "We didn't ask questions," she remembered. Once, when a younger brother arrived, it was her own grandmother who tended to the birth. "I thought Grandma found him somewhere and brought him," she said with a laugh.

Once grown with a family of her own, Granny did not remember any new-mother jitters. She recalled, "I was the happiest girl in the world."

She was uneasy before the first baby came, because just four months earlier her own mother had died in childbirth along with her stillborn twins. The mother was buried with the two babies, one lying at each arm. 'Granny's' uneasy days were short lived. That `happy' young woman was mother to seven more children.

She rocked them to sleep in a handmade rocker and stitched little diapers and baby gowns. In those days, baby boys were dressed the same as girls. "Mine wore dresses 'til they were big enough to walk," said Granny. Then, they wore handmade rompers which were one-piece that buttoned in back with knee length pants.

'Granny's' children never were seriously ill as youngsters, but she remembers her parents tell of a frightful time with her younger brother,

Charlie. He had the whooping cough when he was six weeks old. ``They laid him out... thought he was dead for over an hour,'' said 'Granny'. A neighbor who was there sitting with the family, said, ``that youngun's not dead, he drawed a breath,'' remembered 'Granny'. The neighbor put onions in the fireplace and roasted them for an onion poultice which she lay upon his chest. She squeezed one drop at a time from another onion on to his tongue until he started breathing well again.

Caring for babies in the 1920s required independent thinking and action. Husbands were out early and home late - working to provide necessities. That left women to care solely for the children. They were busy, aside from raising little ones, washing on a wash board, cooking on a wood cook stove, gardening, milking, and so forth.

'Granny' remembers, ``I have took them out and sat them in a box in the shade while I worked in the garden.'' To go outside the house for milking and feeding, 'Granny' would put a gate over the door and leave the babies in the room without a fireplace. She hurried to milk the cow, then ran back inside to check on the children before going to feed the hogs or gather eggs.

Before long, however, she had help. "Earl, from the time he was four years old, he could look after the others," said 'Granny'.

And so it went, the older children helping with the younger ones and assisting their mom and dad until they were all grown. Then, 'Granny' found herself enjoying grandchildren and great grandchildren. She still appears to be `the happiest girl turned granny in the whole world' as she talks about her family — now sixty-four in number.

Viola and Simeon Henry with children,
(l. to r.) Irene, Homer, and Shirley, approximately 1937

Touching History's Mark

Archie Ray Dennis McMahan has numerous vivid impressions left in memories from her young childhood at Mac Cove, later known as Pearl Valley. She briefly touched a mark in history as she touched the hands of a neighbor freed by the Civil War. She lived through heartbreak brought on by diseases of earlier times, and she experienced excitement in a first train ride.

She was born, 1915, to John and Mary Quintina (Tiny) McMahan Dennis who continued the operations of Tiny's father's family farm. McMahan's Great Grandfather, John Tipton Shields, was a doctor, and so were relatives: Dr. Paul Shields, Dr. J. Walter McMahan, and Dr. J. Walter Dennis.

At almost age three, McMahan was lifted onto a horse for one of several rides by the kind hands of a man whose life was changed by the Civil War. Uncle Wash (Washington) Stewart, from a neighboring community, was seventeen years old and a black slave when the Civil War ended, said McMahan, (according to his gravestone.) Just before World War I ended, McMahan recalls walking by lantern light to McMahan School with her family to hear speakers promote the sale of Liberty Bonds.

Her memory reaches into those very early years when she took her first train ride at about age four. The journey to visit McMahan's uncle, Dr. J.W. McMahan in Maryville, began with a buggy ride to the Sevierville train depot (near the present day Sevier Farmer's Co-op building.) At Boyd's Creek area, McMahan recalls that the train stopped and a large sized man wearing a conductor's cap came and said they all must get off the train because a trestle was out. McMahan and her mother joined the other passengers in boarding a freight train on the other side. They rode in a box car seated on boxes into Vestal.

A sad occurrence in McMahan's early years was one experienced by many mountain families, the death of a young family member. McMahan remembers that the well water used for drinking at school became contaminated, and three children became ill with typhoid fever. As their brother Fred, age thirteen, lay sick in bed. the other Dennis children hurried home to tell him of their day at school. Soon afterwards, during the night, their father went to his children and told of young Fred's death. McMahan recalls how the sorrow hushed their

14

mother's singing for a time. Before, she was a happy person, singing as she did her work. As the grief eased, McMahan heard her sister say one day, "listen, Mama's singing again."

That same year, in 1920, McMahan remembered a red letter day for her mother. It was the year of Women's Suffrage, and when election time came, Tiny Dennis put on her best brown suit and left - excited at the thought of her new privilege. McMahan's mother felt it was her duty to vote from that day on; she guessed her mother never missed a day at the polls in her eighty-five year life.

About a year after the death of McMahan's brother Fred, the family lost a favorite shepherd pet dog; one that had been especially dear to him. It was just before the threshers had come with their machines to thresh wheat. McMahan's mother and father had gone to do the evening milking. A mad or rabid dog appeared, and the family feared their shepherd dog, Maggie, was bitten while trying to protect their parents and the cows. At only six, McMahan watched Maggie, wagging her tail, follow along behind a neighbor who had the unpleasant task of shooting the family pet. "I was out in the woodyard just bawling," McMahan said. The little girl went inside so she would not hear the gun shot, and when she got inside she saw her mother quietly working, with tears streaming down her face.

The sad times were few, however, in the Dennis home. Most of McMahan's memories were of pleasant times. She remembers her parents provided a loving home. Her mother prepared meals with variety and made tasty desserts. McMahan came in with her father from the fields and wondered what treat her mother would have that day.

Her parents were loving... yet firm. Once, when she forgot to bring in the stove wood before bedtime, she was awakened at 4:00 a.m. the next chilly morning to bring it from the outside. She never again forgot to carry in the stove wood.

As she talks of those early childhood years, Mrs. Archie Ray remembers a tornado that swept through the area in the early 1920s. It uprooted a pressleaf cedar in their yard and lifted nearby New Salem Church from its foundation and turned it around.

Her brother, Dr. Dennis, once worked with Dr. McCowan of Jefferson City; the two amputated 'Uncle' Dave Dixon's tumored leg in a successful kitchen table-top operation.

She tells of teacher Josie Shepherd who started a little school library with thirty books, probably using pie supper money. And, she thinks of her father's orchard, her mother's homemade hominy and corn meal mush. She remembers sitting on the second seat behind her father, a deacon, at Pearl Valley Baptist Church and the once a year 'May meeting,' for communion. From one vivid memory to another in McMahan's Mac Cove childhood years, this retired school teacher, leaves the impression that those were good years... years to be cherished with memories passed on.

She and husband Fred, living on his family farm in Richardson's Cove, have since raised two sons, Jack and Tommy, and they have four grandchildren and one great grandchild - a family who'll receive her treasured legacy in memories.

Archie Ray
with parents John and Tiny Dennis, 1918

Unending Hours

Sharpening mill rocks, and building a cistern for barn water run-off, and taking wagon wheels into town for repair are entries found in an early 1940's farm journal that records a family's seemingly unending hours of work.

The family, Chester and Melinda Atchley Lane (now deceased) and their two girls and three boys, worked to maintain a 180 acre farm in the Fair Garden community of Sevier County. Chester Lane, educated to the third grade, painted a different picture than that of the modern day farm in his daily recordings.

He filled pages with daily entries of outside conditions. The journal has line after line of entries such as that New Year's day when the farmer 'plowed all day.' He spent many hours tearing down old barns for their lumber on farms that Douglas Dam's waters would soon cover - - places such as Muddy Creek or Swans.

In January he was a busy man: Lane killed hogs, helped render lard, and sold his tobacco in Knoxville; he plowed, went to the stock yard in Newport, into Sevierville, then plowed some more. In February the farmer sharpened mill rocks for his father's corn grinding mill, and he began making preparations for his tobacco season. One day he made a sled to use for hauling brush. He burned the brush to prepare the soil for a tobacco bed then sowed the seeds.

Neighbors stacked hay and sometimes saved it until winter when Lane would take his threshing machine and 'thrush (lespedeza) seed' for them, said his son Earl Lane.

On a 'fair and warmer' day in February Lane cleaned out a cistern. Earl Lane said cisterns were made by digging an area which was three feet square at the top and which widened to 8 feet at a depth of 15 to 18 feet. It was plastered with cement and was sometimes located to catch barn water run-off when it rained; the water was used for drinking and home use. Some placed their cistern near the house, and covered the gutter with cloth to keep out chimney soot.

Folks, then, said farmers should only catch rain water in months that contained "r's" in their spelling. Water caught in the months of May, June, July and August, would get wiggle tails, said Lane.

A lot of back-breaking labor went into the Lane farm. Hours and hours were spent cutting sprouts at Ross Newground or grubbing there or cleaning a fence row. Other daily entries included in the Lane Journal were: 'hauled manure all day,' or 'cut briers on the mountain all day.' Tomato beds were sown and the corn planting began in April. Lane helped neighbors and family in such tasks as building a 'chimley' or planting their corn, or working on their mill dam. He and his 'Pap' put new sills under the barn, and he began harrowing fields.

By May, there was corn to be replanted, tobacco plants and tomato plants to be set and plowing every few days. The Lanes grew their tomatoes and beans for Bushes Canning Factory at Chestnut Hill.

One page of journal entries records sales of milk from Lane's 5 or 6 cows. They were paid $11.04 for two weeks worth of milking by the Pet Milk Plant in Greeneville. At times when the delivery man came to pick up the milk, the Lanes paid another $1.00 payment on the 10 or 12 gallon two-handled milk can. There was an approximate $1.50 haul bill paid to the plant and an additional 4 or 5 cent war tax on the haul bill.

All the clearing and grubbing on the mountain area of the Lane farm resulted in the sales of Cedar wood to Jim Bob Atchley's wood work shop in town. The journal records a $250 dollar payment for the cedar. Lane remembers working in that shop for 10 cents an hour making Coca Cola crates for the Coke plant in Knoxville.

In 1944, Lane sold baby pigs for $5 each and three fattened hogs brought $100. Two acres of tobacco yielded $845 that year. The Lane farm also had income from cattle, wheat, lespedeza seed or hay and some of the first government subsidy AAA checks.

Chester and Melinda Lane and their family made a success of their Fair Garden farm through day after day of work in the fields. Had it not been for Sanders Atchley, a Sevierville banker, their journal could have read differently. When Chester Lane bought his farm and borrowed $3,000 to pay for it, the Depression hit that same Fall. Lane went into town to turn his farm over to the bank, because he knew he did not have the means to make the payments at the time. Atchley would not take the farm; he told Lane to repay it as he could.

Later, as World War II was drawing to a close, some folks began to become restless, said Lane. His family moved to Virginia where land was cheaper. The Lane 180 acre farm sold and brought enough money to purchase 360 acres in Virginia.

Back to Tennessee the Lanes returned, Earl Lane following after his father. Today, he and his wife Catherine live about five miles from the spot where this preacher was born and raised. They have one son - Jim.

Lane reflects over the life of his father, and his strength of character comes to mind. Chester Lane was a man of his word, said his son. As many mountain folks of that day, Lane made trades on a hand shake. When an agreement was made, this man did not back out - not even for more money. He once told a man who offered him a higher amount on a trade that keeping his word was worth more to him than the $500 offered.

Ways of life today are better in many ways than the hand-to-mouth (work hard with your hands for what you put in your mouth) days then. But, leaving in the past the trusting ways of folks who could trade on a hand shake and those who could be trusted is not one of the better ways of today.

A Nickel Paper Poke

"One pail syrup: .65; one gallon potatoes: .25; three boxes matches: .12; one box face powders: .11; and two cakes tub soap: .10" - these are items from a January 1943 grocery bill that was recorded by the Chester and Melinda Atchley Lane family of the Fair Garden community.

A look into their old farm journal gives a peep into the past. It records many every day items purchased from the Fred C. Atchley rolling store which carried much more than groceries. One double blanket, for example, sold for $2.98. A double blanket, explains Lane's son Earl Lane, was a blanket that was about twice the length of the bed. A person slept sandwiched inside it with the folded edge at the foot of the bed. Other non-grocery items recorded in the journal were two pairs of anklets for .58, 1 gallon of oil (for lamps) - .20, 1 pack of envelopes for .05, two bottles of shoe polish for .20, and one pack of 'cleanexes' were .10.

In those early '40s, thread was selling for a nickel; Stand Back headache powders sold for a nickel a pack or six packs for a quarter. Toilet soap and tub soap were two different items, said Lane. Toilet soap was for washing hands or bathing, and tub soap was for washing clothes.

A dime, then, bought many items for a family. For one dime they could purchase one box of oats, a jar of sandwich spread, peanut butter, a loaf of bread, a box of soda, or baking powder. A dime would buy a pack of razor blades, toothpaste, a box of washing powders or a box of crackers. Half that, bought paper pokes (bags), a spool of thread, or a writing tablet, and families could purchase a nickel or dime box of soda.

When the Lanes bought a cake for the preacher on Sunday, they paid a quarter. When they purchased sugar or coffee, it was in quantity - four or five pounds of coffee at approximately 20 or 25 cents a pound, and five, six or twelve pounds of sugar at near 7 cents a pound.

In March, the journal recorded $1.00 for a hundred pounds of crushed oyster shells for the chickens (it helped in their digestion), rouge for eleven cents, two pairs of women's 'step-ins' (or ladies' briefs) for $1.18, and four yards of cloth were $1.20. Items for cooking and cleaning were sold on the rolling store. A broom sold for 29 cents, and a stew bucket was .75. Two big bowls were 50 cents, and two little bowls were .40. One big bread pan sold for a quarter, and a little bread pan was 15 cents.

Several eggs were used to pay on these grocery bills and for other items. One recording after another shows the Lanes sold 30 dozen eggs, 19 dozen or 31 dozen.

Aside from periodic grocery shopping, the Lanes recorded larger purchases in their journal. A pair of glasses, paid for in four payments, was $24.70, and a watch was $5. Slippers or shoes were $2.98. One entry is for a suit for Earl Lane's birthday - a cost of $23.45 from Wade's Store in Sevierville.

Fifty years has made a world of difference between the dime and the dollar. That dime that once bought a pack of razors cannot buy a pack of gum today. Most of the dime items have risen in price more than ten times - the loaf of bread, the box of crackers, the toothpaste. The slippers or shoes, of the same quality, would perhaps be over $50 today. The suit at Wade's store might sell for ten times that amount and more at the mall.

Wages have climbed, as well. The ten cents an hour at the wood-work shop would, today, be at least minimum wage. Perhaps, the greater change, then, since the '40s has been style of living... a style reflected in the comparison of a $2,000 personal computer in a home of the '90's and nickel writing tablet in a home of the 1940's.

Life's Beautiful Patchwork

Cora Alice Ownby Morton was born in 1903 and died 1996. In the year before she aged to 90, this Smoky Mountains area woman could pull far away dates from her memory - the same as if an occurrence happened yesterday.

It was the "20th day of September, 1917", when this young teenager saw her first bear track at the head of Caney Creek on Cove Mountain. She and her sister Emma and her father had gone to pick 6 gallons of huckleberries and 6 gallons of goose berries (to be exact). "I was scared to get a few feet away from my Daddie," she remembered.

Morton recalled several every-day ordinary happenings at her early home on Cove Mountain and later in the Glades community. These occurrences pieced together to make up her long life the same as an old timey patchwork quilt carefully and beautifully comes together.

She was the daughter of James and Ellen Moore Ownby and the great granddaughter of John and Mary Coon Ownby. Moses and Marm McCarter Moore were Morton's maternal grandparents.

From her early school days, Morton recalled carrying (in a syrup bucket) her lunch made of biscuits and jelly, sweet potatoes or corn, or a fried egg and a piece of pie.

"Santy's beard is long and white, and his eyes is very bright," recited Morton from a school Christmas verse that spelled the word 'Christmas.'

Some teachers at that one room Banner School were Ida Clabo, Calvin and Ashley Ogle, Russell Ownby and Russell Watson, and Lewis Clabo. A 1910 school photograph included the following students: Nola King, Clay Ogle, Ezalee and Lou, Arlie and Nole Maples, Charlie, George and Nellie Franklin, Nora Ownby, Lola and Pink Clabo, Pink Maples, Fred and Earnest Lane and Ruth Cole.

Students went to school from August through December, closing a week or so in September to gather in the beans, peas, apples, etc., said Morton, who started her first full year at age 7.

Students wrote on rough paper with penny pencils. She went through the 'chart class,' first through fourth readers and on into 'advanced classes', which in those days, preceded High School.

Morton talked of the sad times such as when her brother died after suffering from typhoid fever and spinal meningitis in 1910 (the year

Banner Church was being constructed)... and the happy times. She experienced salvation at age eleven in a Banner Church revival. And, she later met her future husband, Verless Morton, in that same Banner Church.

The Mortons were of Irish descent, and Verless Morton's maternal grandparents were born in Germany.

Cora Alice was 20 years old and her husband was 32 when they married. Many, then, were married at much younger ages, however, Morton said she wasn't scared at the thought of becoming an 'old maid'.

Verless Morton was away much of the time during their two year courtship and after they were married. He worked several years cutting timber - and had two broken bones to show for his labors from two different logs that rolled over him.

For several more years Verless Morton was employed with the Federal Bureau of Public Roads. He worked a short time as a cook and for a much longer period in a survey party in the building of such roads as those at Newfound Gap, Clingman's Dome and in Cades Cove.

On December 29, 1938, Cora and Verless Morton and almost all of their eleven children moved to the Glades community. They purchased 75 of 150 acres at the homeplace which Cora Morton's Great Grandfather Jacob Evans had willed to her Grandmother 'Sophie' Evans Ownby and 'Sophie's' youngest son Sam Ownby.

The house is around 100 years old.

That old house in the Glades held many memories for Morton and so did her Cove Mountain home as she cared for a large family, many times alone or with the help of her older children.

She sat there in the early 1990's, in a fashionable red dress with her snow white hair pulled back in a bun, and she continued recalling dates and happenings in her life.

Morton remembered the first car she saw, the first airplane and times spent listening to the radio. Of these special times, she would say, "I remember it mighty well."

All the children at Banner School wished they could jump from their studies and run outside as 'K. Rawlings' drove his car to Gatlinburg - the first she had ever seen. They sat staring out the window as he drove by.

"I was over at Bill Maples', over on what they call the Compton Place," remembered Morton as she told of the first airplane she saw, flown by someone named Williams. He landed the airplane at Elkmont.

While Morton was too busy to listen to the radio often, she does remember the gospel singing and the Lone Ranger on the radio at her home in the Glades.

The kind, bright-eyed grandmother told of how two of her brothers, in 1896, hauled lumber from Roaring Fork to Cobb Town (in the Highway 66 area) where it was taken by steam boat to Knoxville.

Another brother Marshall carried the mail from Pigeon Forge to the Sugarlands when he was 13 years old. He was the youngest mail carrier in the United States, she said. Morton's father bid the 'Star Route' off for the period of one year; his son carried the mail for 50 cents a day.

'Brother Dave' and then Bob worked for a pressing club (dry cleaner) in Knoxville.

Morton's talk was interrupted periodically by a soft laugh or a pause in thought as she remembered these earlier times.

Just as clearly as the dates came to mind, so must have the picture memories of her past... pictures of 'dahlies', roses, and snowball bushes... and, memories of children's laughter from inside an abandoned chicken house - play house.

Cora Alice Morton's shared memories are a treasure, the same as her life was a treasure and a pattern of good for those who knew her.

"Where Are The F

There is a low heavy fog hanging o'
gray-green backdrop for the cove below
among their winter feed - fresh rolls of hay, in

Motor sounds of slow moving vehicles through Cades C
the sight of a steady stream of cars ahead are the primary evidences of
modern times in a setting of old.

Vehicles pull to the side of the road and their riders exit at Cades
Cove Missionary Baptist Church, Old Harp music books in hand. Old
time bonnets, full skirts and knee pants have been replaced by today's
Sunday dresses, blue jean shorts, and khaki slacks.

Singers come in and take their place, designated by the part they
sing, forming a square in the front of the church. The partial sunlight
filters in through shimmering panes that date their glass to another
generation. It is the only light on the books' pages in this old building
without electricity. Worn wooden benches hold singers whose voices
echo melodies off sound walls and a floor of mountain wood.

John W. Dunn, from Dry Valley, stands to lead the Old Harp
singers in the opening song - 'Brethren We Have Met To Worship.'
After about the third or fourth song, there's a heavy beat of feet
keeping time to the music. Leaders from around the room take their
turn to stand and sing a number that has, after many Old Harp
singings, become their signature song.

The rhythm inside is as methodical as the rain patting down on the
gravestones outside the church. The leader's right hand lifts and falls,
'up - down - back - and forth', in time to the notes in the book. Each
one has a style of his or her own. Some move about the room, their
arm swinging high and their voice carrying loud - tackling the most
difficult tune. Others stand still, with slight rhythmic motion, still
bringing the voices together to form a rich harmony.

"Let's stay together, this is right beautiful music," encourages one
older leader. Those who attend Old Harp singings seem to agree that
it is. Martha Graham, of Pigeon Forge, said the music is spiritual, and
she loves the blending of the voices without music. Graham's father,
Wiley Franklin, sang bass at Old Harp singings; her mother had
Graham singing at age ten. "Sit here and sing; you're not a runnin' in
and out of the church," she was told. The Franklins went to singings

...cCookville (Gum Stand), Caney, Wears Valley, Coker
...d area), and Huskey's Grove.

...nby, who lived his childhood years at Greenbrier, remem-
...Old Harp singers of his early years. His father, Sam Ownby,
...d Lewis King, Burl Adams, Wil Perryman and Haskew Trevena.
...aid the singings are pretty much the same today as then.

The leaders, then as now, would sound the lead note. Once they
pitched the note with a tuning fork or by ear. Some, today, use a pitch
pipe for the chord, then each section of singers sounds the chord or
their starting note with a 'do', 'me' or 'so', for example. The singers
follow through once, singing the syllables ('do - re - me'), and the
leader calls, 'sing the poetry!'. The second time through, Old Harp
singers sing the words.

Whether folks are caught up in the spirituality of the words or the
sounds of the voices in harmony, there is a definite intensity in the
faces of some of the singers. It is, most likely, the same intensity as
seen on the faces of generations past. Lena Headrick, of Wears Valley,
said Old Harp has been in her family since before they came from
England. Her Great Grandfather Trevena, the family says, 'must have
come (to America) carrying his Bible and his Old Harp book.'

Headrick grew up hearing Old Harp, but really became more
interested when she married an Old Harp singer, Luke Headrick, and
they began attending the singings. In l950, she and her husband, and
a group of about twelve area singers traveled to New York City for a
gathering to present this part of East Tennessee heritage.

Old Harp singings have been in Sevier County for many years.
There is an effort to give rebirth to the schools. The preservation of
'Old Harp' singing is dependant on interest by a younger generation.
And, there is an interest as evidenced by the voices of young leaders
(Sharee Rich began singing at age 7), undaunted to stand before those
older and more sure... And, in the words of a singer's closing prayer
who speaks, 'let us make the rafters ring as those who have before us.'

Singers sound their quiet 'Amen's' to the prayer and begin to make
their way back through the church - shaking hands and hugging old
friends. The rain has stopped, and the sun begins to appear from
behind clouds above. Somewhere in the distance, perhaps, there's a
fawn grazing under the watchful eye of its mother. Cades Cove
Missionary Baptist Church in the Great Smoky Mountains will sit
empty, once again, silent of the voices singing, "Where are the friends
that to me were so dear? Long, long ago. Long, long ago."

The City Meets The Country

The Great Smoky Mountains in early years introduced big city folks to mountain folks as the mountain appeal drew visitors from many far away places.

Five young mountain boys around Gatlinburg could have lived very different lives had they chosen to accept one New York City group's offer.

Otis Williams talks of his younger days in the Forks of the River community just south of Gatlinburg. He tells of how he and four others played music for tips at Edna Sims' Mountaineer Museum.

Almost every evening, the young man, about age nineteen, and his buddies would play for a couple of hours. Foot stomping songs with an old time flavor rang from their instruments.

As the group performed one day, they caught the ear of some New York tourists who were in the music business. The New Yorkers offered to take the five young mountain musicians to New York and pay for music school, as well as their board. The Williams brothers, whose father had died earlier with cancer, were discouraged from leaving home by their mother.

Williams had been working outside the home since he was barely a teenager to help support his family. He dug holes for Shell Oil Company tanks and made five dollars for each hole (which took about a day to dig). In the late 1930's, he made twenty-five cents an hour for digging on the ditch line for the telephone company. He once worked with men who used an old timey scoop made of wood and metal that was pulled by horses to dig the basement for the Gatlinburg Inn.

The Williams boys grew corn on another's farm and gave the landowner one sled load of corn while they kept two sled loads for their family. The workers furnished their own seed and fertilizer.

Living near Fighting Creek and the Little Pigeon, the Williams family and their friends spent much time along the river fishing, swimming in the Igg hole (named for his Grandfather Isaac or Igg Trentham), or gathering drift wood for fires.

Their home, with its clean swept flat yard, was near where the Great Smoky Mountains National Park headquarters building is today. It was a one and a half story weatherboard house, 'L' shaped, with a porch in front and a one story kitchen at the back. Morning glories and cypress vines partly covered the house making it a cheerful place. There were cinnamon vines, as well; these were potato or 'tater vines that grew small 'potatoes' which had the aroma of cinnamon when broken apart. Porch railings were lined with pot flowers in old tin lard buckets and cans.

Williams, his parents James (Jim) Berry Williams from Jones Cove and Elzora Trentham Williams, and their large family lived in the home that was built earlier by their Uncle Isaiah Trentham. Their uncle had once owned a nearby steam powered sawmill which he used for the house lumber.

There was a spring near the house, a log barn, and a chicken house. A foot log crossed over Fighting Creek to their Grandpa Isaac Trentham's home. Today, the tree stands scarred from a chain that held the foot log in place when high waters threatened to wash it down river.

Otis Williams speaks with a warm heart of his days in that house. He is a big man with an easy laugh. He enjoys telling tales of another time the way his Irish ancestors loved to spin yarns. He says his ancestors were the big seafaring Irish, some over six feet tall and big footed. His Grandfather Isaac, a red headed, green-eyed man, told stories of Ireland to his family.

This story told by Otis Williams is a true one from his childhood: Otis or Od's little brother Clyde was three or four years old, when out of the blue, he began asking his mother for sugar. After asking several times, his mother began to wonder what the sweetening was for. She followed her youngster to a big flat rock just outside the kitchen door. There he was with a rattlesnake around his legs. The snake's mouth was open wide and little Clyde was dropping sugar down its mouth.

A frightened mother left to get her husband who loaded his gun and went for the back of the house. Elzora Williams sneaked up behind her little boy and grabbed him by the shirt collar and pants legs. She lifted him straight up and away from the snake while her husband killed the boy's 'pet'. Young Clyde told his father he had been feeding the snake for a few days. He cried and cried because his Daddie killed the pet.

Williams boys and dog, Ted, at the Forks of the River community, 1928:
(l. to r., Isaac Newton, Walker Winfred, Shannon Otis, and David Clyde.

The Real Light

Roadside and hillside praying have almost completely disappeared from Sevier County the way the kerosene lamps and potbellied heaters have vanished from area churches. A zeal for seeing the lost — those unbelieving in Christ Jesus — become Christians has weakened, say four Baptist preachers who have been preaching since around the 1950's.

Jack Bailey, Andy Ball, Melvin Carr, and Clarence Wilson pastor in Sevier County churches. Here, the four talk about old time church meetings and their differences from today.

In earlier times the church buildings were more plain. When Preacher Wilson was a boy and a janitor at Oldhams Creek, he went before service to light the oil lamps and build a fire in the heater.

Bailey relates the story of a young janitor who felt that on one cool Sunday morning it was not cold enough for a fire. He knew, however, that some of the women would think that it was; so he placed a lantern in the stove to resemble a fire. Not a word was said about how cold it was.

When Ball began pastoring, Sevier County had more churches than it had pastors. He pastored three churches at one time. Some of these churches and others held services only one weekend a month. Those with no lamps were restricted to day services, others met on Saturday nights and the following morning or Saturday or Sunday afternoons. Wilson once pastored two churches, and said that he felt as if he pastored one and preached at the other.

As time passed, more became preachers, population grew, and more churches were established.

The Baptists believe ministers are called of God to preach. Some try other ways to serve in the church before submitting to the Lord's will. Wilson says he was in Germany in a truck that hauled troops when he heard a voice, the same as if someone was beside him, telling him to preach. He did, but it was a few years later.

Living in Oak Ridge, Carr was a church deacon when he was called upon to fill in for the pastor. As he felt impressed to become a minister, Carr thought he was ill and went to see a doctor. The doctor found no illness, and the 'sickness' left when Carr announced his call to preach.

Preacher Bailey still recalls his first sermon preached; it was at Walnut Grove and was about Peter's denial of Christ just before His crucifixion. Ball preached his first message at Evans Chapel from the book of Matthew about 'Straight is the gate, and narrow is the way' to Heaven.

In Carr's early years of ministering, he talks of how the mothers and dads would come with tears in their eyes asking him to pray for an unsaved boy. Today, preachers are called on more for counseling, says Wilson. Still, there are some who come to preachers with an urgency to become a Christian, as the man who came to Ball who was on his dozer and asked the preacher to pray with him.

It is, however, unlikely that passers-by will see an old preacher stopping by the fence on his way to revival to kneel down and pray. Preacher Bailey tells about the late John Fox who stopped and crossed the fence to pray, then spotted a sow and her litter of pigs. The sow was a little ill natured; "It was the first time I prayed with one eye on a hog and one on the Lord," the old preacher had told.

Ball laughs about the time he and a group stood up from prayer in a pasture field to find themselves encircled by several cows.

Preacher Bailey, on a more serious note, explains that in earlier times, lay people did more personal work with non Christians at revivals. Ball remembers church goers coming to his house to talk to him about Christ. Neighbors knew each other and witnessing was more personal.

Aside from witnessing and service in the congregation, pastors have their own times for searching the Bible for answers. These four tell of scriptures that sooth their own worries and help others.

For comfort, Carr turns to Matthew 11:28, "Come unto me, all ye that labor and are heavy laden..." He says that verse invites people to come for whatever their need.

"My God shall supply your every need according to his riches in Glory," recites Bailey.

Preacher Wilson says the verse that includes, "My grace is sufficient..." brings comfort.

Preachers have long time been a help to the church members, and church members have long time respected pastors. There was a time when Carr recalls that people fed the preacher the best they had, and many times that was chicken. Carr's daughter, as a child, ate so much chicken that she began to wonder if that was the only food church folks had.

As these Baptists relate the changes over the years, they are firm about the fact that God and the scriptures haven't changed. Ball retells advice once given by Preacher Raymond Hurst: "Study to know the truth, then preach it."

Carr believes from years of study, "As we learn more about the Book, we're more sure that it is fact."

The four consider the present and quote scriptures that sound as if they've just come from an old time revival. They share a love for others and a longing for them to know a loving Christ. Preacher Ball refers to Paul's warning that the day is far spent; it is high time we awake out of our slumber because our redemption draweth nigh.

"Harvest is past, summer is ended and we are not saved," (Jeremiah 8:20) quoted Carr; and Wilson said that his prayer is for God to send a spiritual awakening in Sevier County.

Bailey's one sentence message for the present: "Repent or perish."

These scriptures and verses of "O Why Not Tonight" have stopped filtering from the Sugarlands church services as in Carr's boyhood days. No longer are church steeples accompanied by chimneys for wood heaters, and community schools do not march students into daytime revivals, two and three weeks long. The kerosene lamps, too, are gone, said Bailey, "but the real light is still there."

Preacher Jack Bailey
baptizes a Mt. Zion church member in the 1950s.

Christmas Sparkle

To see a child's eyes light up as they open presents at Christmas time is a joy for parents.

Children of the Great Smoky Mountains in the 1920s and before talk of Christmas toys and everyday games that were far different than those of today. These plain, simple toys brought the same sparkle and that same joy because they were created with ingenuity, enjoyed with a vivid imagination, and given in love.

Iva Franklin Campbell, tells of reading on a lot on cold winter days — books such as 'The Little Women,' that were Christmas gifts sent from family out West.

Santa, she said, would leave a big orange, a stick of candy and an apple in their stockings, and her mother bought and made clothes for gifts under the tree. She remembers one Christmas doll that would open and close its eyes.

Her mother's family sent cloth for dresses, and her Grandpa sent a big box of shelled out English walnuts, pecans and filberts (the hazel tree nut), from his farm. An uncle who lived in Idaho sent a five gallon can of creamed alfalfa honey — a real treat that lasted the entire winter.

Snow cream and snowmen were a part of winter fun. "We would hook up the horse and Papa would take us in the sled and ride around in the snow," said Campbell.

Throughout the year, she and her three sisters played with paper dolls, played hopscotch, pushed a scotch wheel, and played jack rocks. "Mama said she'd get so tired of hearing us say, 'no slips, no slips.'" Campbell said they called out 'no slips' if they dropped the ball or missed the jack rock so they would not have to give up their turn.

In the summer time, the children climbed trees at their Mill Creek farm. One sat on one limb and pretended to play the piano on the limb in front. The others sang, and the group had 'church.'

Pearl Clabo Huskey recalls the little red rocking chairs that sat under the tree for herself and each of the Clabo children when she was only three or four. The little handmade rockers were special, because Huskey said they never received store bought toys.

A good imagination and a catalog provided day after day of fun for Huskey and her sister Lily at their Caney home. "We had the most fun getting out and making moss play houses," she said. They cut out a family of paper dolls from the catalogs given them by their Aunt Lily Houser. Their mother made furniture out of pasteboard boxes, and she helped them gather the moss for the imaginary doll house. Huskey and her sister made a fireplace out of sticks, and their house was complete for the dolls that were named with their own family names.

Martha Franklin Graham remembers the corn shuck and rag dolls for Christmas. Her mother made the rag dolls with buttons for eyes and a string for the mouth. The dolls were stuffed with cotton; they had legs made from the knit material used for making underwear and hair made with crocheting or knitting thread.

Apples, oranges and candy were in the stockings and under the tree, and new shoes were received at Christmas time. "One of us would get store bought jack rocks and Clark (her brother) would get marbles."

All year round, the Franklins played with toys such as the spool crawler, many made by her brother. They had fun with car tires and made stilts by attaching cans to long pieces of wood, or to laurel walking sticks, or straight bean sticks. The stilts were secured around the legs with belts.

The Franklins used a stiff wire with a hook at the end (some used spools) for pushing a small wagon wheel rim called a scotch wheel.

Blanche Roberts Ogle, whose birthday is on Christmas day, remembers a special Christmas doll that she carried for a long time. Her mother made the doll from a piece of stove wood when Blanche was about age seven. The doll was padded with cotton that her mother had grown. It had a dress and bonnet, and the doll's arms and legs were made with corn cobs, also padded with cotton.

She recalls someone gave her bright red nail polish when she was five, and she remembers the marbles (marvels) and dominoes. Other times, the Roberts children of Jay Ell swung on grape vines and dropped into a hay stack, then had to be pulled out. They jumped rope with grape vine ropes or ropes from their Father's farm. Her brother once was rolling his cousin inside a tire when he let go, and the cousin rolled into the river.

Mintha Trentham Cook, an early Elkmont resident, received store bought and handmade dolls for Christmas toys. Her brothers got wooden wagons and wooden sleds. Her own children had home made replicas of the Little River Lumber Company log loaders and skidders. Her children also played with a 'jumping Jack', a wooden marionette that was attached to a stick. The children sat on one end of a paddle and patted the other end to make 'Jack' dance.

Annie Faye Walker Kerr played with one of the earliest versions of a toy oven. At age five, her father bought a toy cast iron cook stove. It had a front door that opened and little eyes and a leaf to place pans on. She was three when she received her first store bought doll made of a material similar to chalk. Kerr remembered the toy china dishes she received for Christmas and the dishes she played with that were made from zinc canning lids or broken grown-up dishes.

This White's Community resident enjoyed boy games as much as playing with dolls and her stove. She played rollie hole or rollie holie — a game of marbles in the dirt.

Kerr played house in her Grandpa's woods. She and the other children lined off a playhouse with rocks around a tree and used the tree roots for chairs. They swept the house with cedar limb brooms.

Other early toys and games of the Smokies included tag games of ante (or Annie) over and kick-the-can. Children made 'Jacob's ladder' and cups and saucers with a looped thread, and they looped a piece of thread through two holes in a button to make a spinning toy. A buzzing or zizzing toy was made by attaching a thin flat piece of rich pine to a thread and whirling it around.

Children made bulger wagons (a board with wooden wheels that was guided by placing the feet on the front axle and ridden down slopes), stick horses, stick reindeer, wooden guns, and wooden flips (slingshots), and they made shadows on the wall at night.

These everyday toys and games and the special Christmas toys are still remembered by the Grandmas and Grandpas of today. The sparkle almost seems to reappear as they talk about those playful, happy times as children.

A Grassy Field

SPENCE FIELD: "A man named Spence was the first to settle here. He was took with this big grassy field and I reckon he liked it cool. Thar's plenty of breeze up here, breeze enough to turn you over and start you rollin' down the mountain," said Sam Cook in 'The Great Smoky Mountains,' by Laura Thornborough, (UT Press).

The Spence Field spoken of here is a grassy bald reached by trail that begins at the Cades Cove picnic area, and its first settler was James Spence, born 1812. Spence's great grandson Mynatt (age 74 in 1995) who lives near Richardson's Cove, tells family stories about this frontiersman. He and his own grandson, Michael Spence have pieced together rich heritage recollections — of times when pioneers were settling the Smokies from far away places.

Leaving his Holland homeland with his Irish wife and a hog rifle and powder horn, James Spence settled in Spence Field (by way of North Carolina,), said Mynatt Spence, on top of what early settlers called the Great Smoky Mountains Divide. Today, the Appalachian Trail crosses through the middle of Spence Field.

Spence homesteaded on the land, and may have never owned a written document to prove it, said Mynatt Spence. The only written records found to date show the first land grant entry in 1830 to someone else; however James Spence is listed as a chain carrier for the second land entry survey in 1838. His son Robert was later recorded (for eviction) in a Spence Field land suit case, according to information in National Park archives.

This grassy homeland owned by the Spences became grazing grounds for cattle in the 1800s recalled the late J.B. Waters at age 91 in a Gatlinburg Press article, 1975. "My father was one of several who took their cattle to the top of the Smokies on April 15 and returned them on September 15," he said. "Settlers had been coming to Spence's cabin long before; most of them traveled with a dog and colored slaves. They were equipped with a flintlock rifle and an axe. They usually located near a good spring and brought garden seed, cleared a portion of land and raised vegetables," the article read.

This annual April cattle drive left an impression on a young boy, according to the article. "You could hear cowbells ringing and dogs barking throughout the land. I have seen as many as 300 cattle pass my home in one day," (Waters) recalled.

For those traveling or herding across Old Smoky, Spence had stockades for their cattle. He charged five cents a head for the cow feed and a place to sleep, and five cents a person for lodging, supper and breakfast, said Mynatt Spence.

The Spence cabin was also used for other individuals — as a haven when someone was running from justice, said Spence. In return for this haven, the criminals helped Spence clear the land. Spence's cabin was located astride the Tennessee, North Carolina line (state boundaries have since changed.) Fugitives, then, would not be arrested if they crossed state lines, said Spence. When 'the law' from Tennessee came looking for their prisoners, all they had to do was step into another room into North Carolina, and vice versa.

Spence Field's cabin residents were visited by others from outside their mountaintop region as the Civil War approached. When it did, it took its toll on the Spences, their son James was killed in battle.

It was said by Mynatt Spence's Father, Andrew, and Uncle Will that men of the Civil War would cut off the fingers or hands of a young man who would grow up and later fight for the opposing side. Spence's ancestors dressed his Grandfather Robert Spence, a young man with long hair, in a dress to prevent this from happening to him.

Civil War battles gave the elder James Spence (who was probably a Union Soldier) the nickname, Bull of the Woods, said Spence, because he was hard to catch. The soldier would go off to battle and return home to rest and heal his wounds. Once, enemy soldiers came looking for him; his wife was busy piling tree sprouts and brush on a brush pile as they searched Spence Field. They never found Spence who was hiding in a hollow place inside the brush pile. It continued to be his hideout when he was home; his wife carried food to him there.

Spence tells how his Great Grandmother, Caroline, was approached by soldiers from time to time. Once, they took her horse that she used in making crops, and they gave her an old one, battleworn and cut up with bayonets. She doctored the horse until she could use it for farming. On the last, said Spence, they killed the family cow.

Perhaps, Caroline Spence had had enough when a soldier loaded corn from the crib into his sled and started to leave. In an effort to save the corn (farmers could scarcely live without corn), she turned the sled over on him and smothered him to death, said Spence.

The Civil War came and ended, and James and Caroline Spence died. After their death their son Robert moved to Alabama; he married, and he and his wife had one son, Alexander. Robert Spence's wife died of the 'child bed fever,' (fever that resulted from infection after a birth), so he left his infant son for her parents to raise and moved back to Tennessee. He visited his son twice each year. Robert Spence remarried to Martha Lowe, and the two of them set up housekeeping at The Sinks or White Oak Sinks near Tuckaleechee in Townsend.

The Spences later settled on Blalock Creek near Richardson's Cove and left behind their legacy: the Spence name on a grassy mountaintop in the Great Smoky Mountains.

Today, Mynatt Spence sits in his Richardson's Cove home overlooking the river, remembering earlier days, different ways. Cattle herders climbing to Spence field have been replaced by folks visiting a National Park. Still, some things remain the same. Evening low lying fog begins to blanket the earth as whisps of smoke wind from cozy mountain homes. Tiny white caps form where rain swollen rivers dash cold water against the rocks. Barns are filled to running over with hay for winter livestock feed. Brightly colored leaves, dulled by the absence of the sun sinking behind mountains, fall the same today in Richardson's Cove as 160 or so years ago on Spence Field.

Elkmont Paths

Three women sit and recall their different paths in life that came together in the Teaster family - paths that crossed common ground in the Elkmont area of the Great Smoky Mountains.

Iva Teaster Whaley was born in the Webbs Creek area of Sevier County in 1915. Myrtle Cogdill Teaster, born in 1916 at Sunburst, North Carolina, was married to Whaley's brother Woodrow Teaster. Lela Reagan Teaster, another sister-in-law, was married to Bruce Teaster. She was born in 1924 at Fighting Creek near Elkmont.

Logging jobs in the Great Smokies employed many people from a broad area around the mountains. These three share the stories surrounding their lives at Elkmont and before.

Lela Teaster's parents were Alfred and Frances Ownby Reagan. Her father worked for the Little River Lumber Company and helped in the construction of Highway 441 across the Smokies. She remembers her mother's story that brings to mind the old 'Guardian Angel' pictures. Teaster's parents were hoeing potatoes, and they left her, at age three or four, on the other side of Little River with her younger sister, Della, who was barely walking. "Mama was hoeing to beat the band to get back to me and Della. She turned around and saw us walking across a big high foot log over the river," said Teaster. Her father told his wife, "Don't you say a word, just go and meet them." He froze in his tracks and waited until the two little girls, holding hands, were safe across.

The two Reagan girls started young doing things together. Lela Teaster remembers how they stood on dynamite boxes to reach the stove and cook for their mother who was ill much of the time with asthma. She guessed the boxes came from her father's work clearing for the highway across the Smokies.

Myrtle Teaster recalls a sad time in her family's life before she met the Teasters. She was about four, around 1920, when the flu epidemic hit Sunburst, North Carolina. Teaster's mother would lie in bed and look out on the hill at the graveyard; she watched as four and five people a day were carried there to be buried.

Teaster's father was employed by 'the works', a logging operation at Sunburst. The company hired black people to set up tents, cook, work and bury the dead during the epidemic, she remembered. Her entire family had the flu; a younger brother and sister died and were buried the same day. They were buried in coffins probably made the same as others in that day - from boards in the ceiling (Teaster said because these were dry boards). She has memories of being lifted by her dad to look in at the two.

Iva Teaster Whaley has roots in North Carolina, as well. Her mother, Jane Hicks Teaster, was born in Haywood County, and her father William (Bill) Counsel Teaster was born in eastern North Carolina. Harmon's Den, just off Interstate 40 near the Hartford exit, was named for her grandfather Harmon Teaster, she said. Harmon Teaster followed logging jobs around a widespread area. He had his own team of steers which he used as he cut and hauled trees.

Around 1905, Harmon Teaster died when his saw mill exploded and capped down over him in Del Rio, Tennessee. His son, Whaley's father, went there for the burial; the men made a coffin from lumber at the mill and buried him nearby. Bill Teaster carved an H on a stone and placed it for his father's headstone at his grave so far away from his birthplace.

Whaley tells her parent's story of how they moved to Elkmont from North Carolina.

They began their walk early in the morning, her father carrying what clothes and covers he could and her mother holding an ax in one hand and a baby in another. The four small children probably carried small bundles along, too. They arrived at Elkmont at night; somewhere along the way, Whaley's, mother had gotten tired and her father had told her to lay down the ax and he would come back for it later. When the family arrived, they found a large building with shavings all around. They piled the shavings in one corner, placed their covers on them and fell asleep. The next day new neighbors brought items for the family to assist until they could begin furnishing a new home.

Myrtle Teaster tells that the first items her father-in-law, Bill Teaster, bought were tin cups to drink from for each of the family members. His first job at Elkmont was working on the road that would bring the train to Elkmont.

The family lived in the center of Elkmont with workhands all around. Whaley's mother had earlier told that she was sitting in her house churning butter and cooking supper when she heard a racket on the rooftop. Her house had caught fire and workhands were on top removing boards and 'dousting the fire' before she knew there was a fire.

Whaley's father bought a farm at Webb's Creek and moved his

family there around 1915 when she was born. Farming could not support his family, so he walked every Sunday back to Elkmont to work and returned home on Saturday. About six years later, the Teasters returned to Elkmont because the Webb's Creek farm could not provide for the family. Bill Teaster worked for 'Uncle Levi Trentham' who owned a lot of land around Elkmont. Teaster logged and drove a team of oxen for Trentham. Once, when a huge log was cut across the mountain and horses could not pull it out, Ezra Ownby and Bill Teaster or 'Pap' were called for.

"He (Teaster) took two yokes of steers, backed the steers up and hooked to the log. Pap had a big black snake whip that he popped in the air over the steers' backs. It sounded like a gunshot," said Whaley. The animals started out on their knees and began pulling. Once they started, 'Pap' wouldn't let them stop until the log moved.

Myrtle Teaster remembers her move to Elkmont in the early 1920s. Her Grandpa Ave Cogdill had died and her Grandmother, who operated a store there, kept writing for Mrytle's father to bring his family and come live with her on Mitch Branch at Elkmont. Teaster's father, Nip Cogdill, worked on the train at Little River Lumber Company and traveled for a year at a time to other logging operations to operate a steam shovel. She didn't know him when he returned home, and once remembers running in the house to hide from the stranger outside.

The three women with Elkmont pasts continue to laugh and talk through the morning telling of awful tasting caster oil with turpentine drops, and recalling some of the same neighbors and old time revivals.

They have enough memories of Elkmont to fill many morning hours recalling good times and bad, happy times and sad.

William Counsel Teaster
and his team of oxen used in logging around Elkmont.

41

Yellow Spring Hollow

Doyle Gibson, born in 1911, was raised at the foot of Bluff Mountain in Yellow Spring Hollow near a sulfur spring that once ran more true to its name. The spring, which was a site for church picnics, ran regardless of the dry weather.

He sits, today, recalling his boyhood days at Yellow Spring. Gibson talks of school, community socials, music, and the Great Depression.

He attended school at Black Oak, a white weather board one-room building on Goose Gap road. Earlier, his father - Sam Wiley Gibson (born early 1870), went to a log school building at Black Oak Grove. By 1925, the four room Whites School, a consolidation of Black Oak, Sugar Loaf and Whites, was constructed. It was the site for Saturday night literary society gatherings in the 1930's which included readings, comedies, and debates. Uncle Will Pickel, a well-read man, was noted in those parts for his Saturday night debates. He and school principal Hubert Tarwater and Ted Davenport debated such topics as the Monroe Doctrine, for example.

Lavator Walker, Ector Rule, Harold Baker and Gibson sang as a quartet at the meetings. Gibson played the mandolin for a string band, and Lawrence Lewelling or Gibson's brother James was the fiddler. Sam Matthews and Beck Lewelling played guitar. The fiddler started a tune, and the others joined in. Melodies with unknown names from the past, perhaps from England or Ireland, were played.

Another musician in the Gibson family was Doyle Gibson's Grandpa Jasper. He rode an old gray mule all over the county leading Old Harp singings. Folks would call a page number from the song book, and the singer could lead the shaped notes by heart (from memory).

Gibson thinks of those entertaining nights at the school, and of his high school years, and he remembers a period that outranked both. It was a highlight in his young life, a trip to Fort Oglethorpe, Georgia. The boy's primary transportation had been his walking shoes or a horse and buggy that he rode to Sevier County High School. While a teenager, he boarded a bus to Chattanooga and a military truck to the Georgia 30-day citizen military training camp.

At the rifle range, he was the best in the whole troop, until they gave him an old World War I rifle too unfamiliar. When Gibson returned home, his friends asked all sorts of questions. "Everybody thought I'd been around the world. I thought I had, too," he said.

The same as in many Tennessee self-sufficient families, the Depression came and went without as much hardship on the Gibson's as those off the farm. "It was rough, but we lived right on through it," said Gibson. He remembers 1928 as being the last pretty good year before the Depression. People scrimped, they sold butter and eggs, but nobody went hungry. The government provided 25 pound bags of flour to help during the Depression, but Gibson said his father was too proud to take any. Sometimes, they ate corn bread for breakfast, because they could not afford flour.

Gibson's mother, Mary Ann Keeble (pronounced Kibble), 'came into a little money' as an inheritance. His Grandfather James T. Keeble died of the consumption or tuberculosis at thirty-three, and his Union soldier pension (about ten or twelve dollars a month) was sent to his family. Some of those savings were for Gibson's knee pants or a couple of his little dress suits which he wore and thought that he was fine.

"We lived on a little one-horse farm (about a hundred acres)," said Gibson. Almost everything folks ate was grown on the farm. Gibson trapped rabbits and sold them for fifteen cents which he used for cigarette money. He made a rabbit box for trapping. The box had a bored hole in the top with corn placed underneath. When the rabbit went in for the corn it tripped a trigger and the box lid fell down catching the animal. The rabbits were sold to Ed Baker's or Wade Johnson's rolling store (a hack pulled by a team of horses). The rolling store drivers took the rabbits to Knoxville and sold them for food for a quarter.

As Gibson grew older, he began to look for better ways to make a living. In the early '40s he and his wife Dee Thomas Gibson moved to a town near Cleveland, Ohio to work, then returned in 1944. They raised their son and daughter, Jerry and Sandra, about two miles from Yellow Spring Hollow. The family now includes five grandchildren and three great grandchildren.

Today, Gibson is retired from the Aluminum Company of America, and his retirement years have been spent mowing the lawn, working a little garden, fishing with his grandson, and making music every now and then.

The Mountaineer

"The days never were long enough to get all the playing or working done" when Lucinda Oakley Ogle was growing up in the Smokies early in this century.

Laughter breaks into her stories as Ogle, born in 1909, recalls her lively youth and courting years. In a home surrounded by flowers, ground squirrels, gray squirrels and hummingbirds, this mountain woman tells of days past with the same enthusiasm used by her storytelling father, Wiley Oakley.

Before her teen years, Aunt Lucinda lived above her maternal grandfather Noah Bud Ogle's place by LeConte Creek or Mill Creek at the foot of Mount LeConte. She still pictures the wooden trough carrying ice cold spring water down to her Granny's back porch into two tubs hewn from a tree. As a child she and her brothers and sisters played with flutter mills turned by water coming out of a spout in the branch.

She talks about her father's old-fashioned apple trees and remembers the sweet smell of the pretty crab apple blossom at her home there on Bull Head.

The good Lord put all those fish in the streams, Aunt Lucinda said, because there was always plenty for the taking. They supplied a big portion of the Oakley family diet. One man took more than his share, though - reckoned the Oakley children. They and other kids living along Mill Creek had a plan for when they saw him coming with his fishing pole after a good rain. They'd rock a fishing hole, then send a runner upstream to warn someone else so they, too, could rock the hole and save the fish for the families along the creek.

Aunt Lucinda's father and his friends would sometimes walk to Fish Camp near Elkmont to fish. They returned home with flour pokes full of trout wrapped in birch leaves to keep them fresh.

Almost everywhere he went, Wiley Oakley was telling tales or finding humor in everyday conversations. Aunt Lucinda said he liked to use big words; he would learn new ones and teach them to his children. She remembers when he gathered them up and taught such words as "r-h-o, ro, d-o, do, d-e-n, den, d-r-o-n, dron, rhododendron," which he spelled and sounded out in a chant.

Once Wiley Oakley was asked, "how many kids you got?"

To this he replied, "I've not counted lately, but when I last counted,

I had an even dozen."

Aunt Lucinda's father told bedtime ghost stories to his children; today, she has tales of her own. "Going into Elkmont, you used to go by a graveyard. There was an old house by the graveyard, and some folks told this young boy they would give him five dollars if he would sleep there at the house. After accepting the dare, the boy was sitting on the porch in the night when he heard a hoot owl calling, 'hooo, hooo, hooo.'"

The story continues, "A white thing came swooshing down towards him. He jumped up and ran harder than he'd ever run before - the white thing running right along with him. When the boy could run no further, he sat down, breathing hard. 'Boy, we had us a good race, didn't we!' exclaimed the ghost.

'Yeah,' the boy answered, 'you let me rest awhile, and I'll make another good stretch on down the road!'"

The boy was later asked if he really did see a 'haint'. He told that, 'no', he had not; he had concocted the entire story so he could keep his five dollars. He did admit to being afraid and running all the way home.

In her youth, real life could be frightful enough without the ghost stories. Aunt Lucinda tells of a time when the family had just killed a hog, and the smell of the fresh meat lured a panther to the house. She still remembers the sound of the wild animal, one similar to a scream-ing woman. Her mother, home alone with three children, closed the house up and built a fire in the chimney to keep the panther from coming down inside the house. She fired shots out the shuttered window in an effort to frighten it away.

Rebecca Ogle Oakley, the following morning, made a baby carrier with a sheet that was similar to those that Indian women used for toting a baby on their backs. She carried her smallest daughter and a gun away from the house - with a young son on one side and Aunt Lucinda hanging onto her apron on the other. The four made their way two miles to her sister's home at the head of Baskins Creek, with the panther following behind.

Lucinda's mother must have been handy with a gun; she shot or chopped with a hoe the snakes that the little feisty dog didn't scare off. Copperheads and rattlers were the only poisonous snakes around, said Aunt Lucinda. Others such as the puffing adder (the flat head or blowing adder) puffed its flat head and blew as a means of protection.

A mountain girl learned quickly where the dangers were and how to avoid many. (Bears, she noted, were not dangers because they were killed for meat about as quickly as they were seen.) Some dangers, however, were invited. Once, Aunt Lucinda and a cousin were

45

playing house. The cousin was accustomed to dipping snuff, but Lucinda wasn't, so when she tried a dip of sweetened snuff she swallowed some. As she went limp from the strong tobacco, her cousin quickly ran to tell her mother that Lucinda had died. Lucinda's aunt took the cream skimmings off milk and eased some into her mouth. "When she got me urpin', I got well soon," she said with a laugh.

Another occasion, Aunt Lucinda and her sister were cleaning two boarders' rooms in their home, the John Whaley place. They saw several fruit jars of corn liquor sitting around and decided to try some. She was later told this was the worst thing they could have done, drinking from the jar, because the fumes intoxicate before a drink is ever taken. The two became giggly and went out and climbed an apple tree. They could not get down and would not ask for help for fear they'd get a switching. They stayed in the tree giggling until they were able to climb down.

Days of youthful pranks soon turned to courting days. At 15, young Lucinda received a letter from Earnest Ogle, a man from the Sugarlands who had been by her house on a bear hunt. She didn't have 2 cents with which to reply. So, Crockett Maples, the horseback riding mail carrier, offered to carry the letter without going through the post office. The carrier justified his actions, saying Earnest was up there pining away waiting to hear from Lucinda.

At first, Lucinda's father disapproved because some folks in that area fooled with moonshine, he said. After some coaxing by Maples, her father finally agreed. At 17, Ogle proposed marriage to Lucinda. She wanted to go away to school, but when her beau told her he would leave and she would never see him again, she changed her mind and married. "I was afraid I'd have as many kids as Mama," she said.

The couple started their lives together with a few meager belongings and a red and white spotted calf her mother gave them. The calf wasn't fattening fast enough, thought Aunt Lucinda, so she fed her more. She fed her so much the young calf died. Her father-in-law took the hide from the calf and tanned it. Many years later, he gave Aunt Lucinda a beautiful banjo head made from the hide. It gave musical enjoyment for years, she said.

Aunt Lucinda talks of the little red calf and her start into marriage, a life far different from today's. She could continue until many pages are filled, because this is one woman who is proud of sharing her mountain heritage. She loves being called a mountaineer, but not a hillbilly. "Mountaineers work," she explains.

Earnest and Lucinda Oakley Ogle

Opening The Doors

"Little girl, my life's delight,
  Skipping happily and so light,
Comes and climbs into my lap,
  Curls herself to take a nap,
Winds herself around my heart;
  I'm hoping this will never part.
Protector, guardian, I must be,
  Teaching things that she should be.
She's my treasure, my concern;
  Truths I'll teach so she can learn."
  Lula Watson, 1979

Miss Lula began teaching school in the mid 1930's, and somewhere along the way, educating others and teaching her own little girl, she saved special memories for poetry as in the verse above.

School doors swing open each year creating new doors of opportunity that were yet to be thought of by Lula Houser Watson's students in her early teaching years. Students walking into those classrooms knew a different educational world than the one their grandchildren would know.

At the beginning of the school year, Watson would receive a broom (she was responsible for the cleaning, too), a water bucket and dipper, a box of chalk, and two erasers per room. She received oil for oiling the classroom floors, but no books - the students brought their own.

Some of the children, in the early years, came to school without books, pencils or paper. Those who had books and supplies shared with those who had none, and Mrs. Watson left spaces on the corners of the blackboard on which they could do their written work. She saved every scrap of her own paper and picked up used papers discarded by students to save for those without any.

The twenty-five year old felt at home in her first teaching assignment at the small Williamsburg country school. She taught the last half of the school year beginning December 1936. There were two eighth graders, one seventh grader, a couple of sixth graders, and more on down to first grade. She was at home there, because it was similar to the schools she had attended as a girl.

Earlier, her own door of opportunity for education had been opened by Preacher Joel Carr, a friend of Watson's father, also a Baptist preacher. Carr had spoken to Mayme Grimes Hill (principal at Smoky Mountain Baptist Academy) about two girls, Miss Lula and Miss Gladys, her sister, who needed an education. Mrs. Watson said after eighth grade she did not know the opportunity for high school existed until Carr came to visit her father.

Hill made it possible for many area students to receive an education through securing assistance from other Baptists. Miss Lula recalls one Sunday School class from Washington, D.C. that sent money for students.

She completed four years at Smoky Mountain Baptist Academy in a graduating class of six. The Dean of Mars Hill Baptist College in North Carolina opened another door for the two Houser girls. He and his wife provided room and board for the two in exchange for assistance in their home with four small boys. Miss Lula and Miss Gladys received a professional certificate in the study of education. The girls' high school principal Hill had suggested that course of study when they entered the Baptist college.

After the young school teacher left Williamsburg, she was the only teacher hired to teach in her community at Oldham's Creek. It was 1937, the same year she married Albert Watson. She remembers going to the Superintendent's office for her handful of supplies. While there, the Superintendent announced that the county could add one more school teacher. The school that could maintain the best attendance average for the first month of school would add a new teacher. (Oldham's Creek had been a two teacher school in years past before attendance had dropped.)

She returned home and told everyone she saw and then announced the superintendent's offer in Sunday School. She asked anyone with children to send them to school on Monday. Seventy-five community children, on the average, showed up most days that first month. Mrs. Watson said she reminded them everyday to return the next day. They all worked together in their assignments, and those who completed lessons first assisted the others. "They all knew it was for a purpose," remembered the teacher, and Oldham's Creek got their second school teacher, Blanche Blalock.

Mrs. Watson continued for many years in the classroom. Her teaching strengths may have been in her diversity, her love for children, and her wish to instill a knowledge of 'right from wrong.' Her enthusiasm for art and music was shared in her teachings, and she had daily devotions and prayer. In Miss Lula's years in the one and two room schools, teachers were expected to be many things to all students. They had more flexibility over their own methods of teaching, and most earned a respect that was next to that of parents and religious leaders.

There must have been a sweet sense of satisfaction in working with students for four or eight years and watching them grow and change as the years passed. Still, Watson remembers the walks home from school thinking, "There's so much more I should have done, if I had had more time."

Students of the thirties, forties, and fifties... walking into rooms that smelled of oil on wood and warm late summer breezes through open windows, may have been in a different world of learning. However, educators of those and earlier years put the wheels in motion for opening doors of greater opportunity for future generations.

Oldham's Creek School children playing marbles, 1950

Miss Lula, 1944

Ma's Tales

Not too many years after the close of the Civil War, Corintha (Rintha or Rinthie) Louisa Maples Watson was born at her Grandfather Israel Carver's house in Big Cove near Cherokee, North Carolina. Kate Watson Beck, her daughter, remembers 'Ma' as a fun loving person who seldom had idle hands. The stories Rinthie told her children and grandchildren brought laughter for many years.

One story, for example, was of Beck's Granny Jane on a cow hunt. Late in the evening, Jane had gone looking for the cows to be milked. She had to search way into the mountains as the evening grew late. Her brother, Aden (Adrian) Carver, began to worry when she did not return home and he began hearing the sounds of a panther (or painter) somewhere in the woods. Jane was hearing the same wild animal as she was bringing the cows home.

Uncle Aden's worry sent him looking for Jane. He soon saw the cows headed in his direction, and his concern was replaced by an idea for some fun. The mischievous man stepped behind a tree, out of sight. Jane, meanwhile, watched as her cows shied away from that tree in the distance. She may have suspected the panther was hiding there, so when 'Uncle Aden' jumped from behind the tree, she nearly lost her wits in fright.

Later, in those same North Carolina mountains, Rinthie (named from Corinthians in the Bible) had her own cow huntin' tale. 'Ma' had gone to hunt the cows when she walked up to a chestnut tree that had broken over, said Beck. She stood on the tree, looking through the woods. As she happened to look down, she saw there below her feet was an Indian hunter lying still as the tree. The unexpected sight gave Rinthie a scare at that time and a laugh later.

Smoky Mountain folks, in earlier times, were sometimes afraid of the blowing mountain winds and hard rain storms. When Rinthie was six or so, she was out walking in the mountains as a hard wind began to blow. "She put her arms around a tree the best she could and said, 'Lord, don't let the wind blow me away,'" said Beck. The wind continued, she held on and repeated, 'Lord, don't let the wind blow me away!' After the third time: 'Lord, don't let the wind blow me away,' the wind continued. The little girl decided, 'well, the Lord just don't care nothing about me.' He did. She survived the wind and

51

lived until her 89th birthday.

The people of that day had reason for fear of the hard storms, the panthers, and the bears — a way of mountain life. They were, however, not reluctant about asking for help from above.

Rinthie never wasted time fretting over the dangers. She even found time amidst the long hours of work to make her own fun. 'Ma' was married and living at Oldham's Creek in the days when people rocked houses. The White Caps (a band of hooded men who sought their own justice) threw rocks at houses as a warning of more severe punishment if the person living inside did not 'mend their ways.'

'Ma' lived in a house that was joined to another with a 'dog run' or breezeway. She hid and began throwing clods of dirt and rocks onto the roof of the adjoining house. Her sister-in-law Lizie and Lizie's nephew were inside, afraid, because of the White Cap stories they had heard. The nephew boldly shouted, "You better stop that, or I'll fill you full of shot!"

'Aunt Lizie' called out and asked, "Rinthie, is somebody rocking your house?"

"No," Rinthie replied - and probably with a laugh, "but if they throw anymore rocks you just come on over and stay with me."

'Ma' was a petite woman with black hair that was cut only once. She was so small, in fact, that her size once helped her avoid trouble. She was up in a tree, shaking out the mulberries, when a neighbor's hogs came and started eating the berries as they fell.

Rinthie yelled at the hogs to run them away. When they would not leave, she said, "I'll get you to goin'". She slid down the mulberry tree, grabbed up a rock, and threw it at the hogs. Rinthie killed one of the hogs with that one rock. Just a young girl, Rinthie was afraid for anyone to know what she had done, so she pulled the hog into the bushes. Later, the neighbors had found their dead hog and came to find its killer. They asked Rinthie if she had seen their hogs, and 'yes,' she had, she said.

The father of the family she was staying with (not knowing the truth) told his neighbor, "Rinthie couldn't have killed it; she couldn't have drug it away."

It may not have looked as if the small girl could tackle such a big task; but, according to Beck, that was her 'Ma's' way. She grew up in a hard life, but always found a way to make life work and to make it more enjoyable.

A Walk In Her Shoes

Most older people of the Great Smoky Mountains once knew women in each community that could have 'walked in these shoes.'

The 'shoes' carried the feet of a woman who loved the Lord, her family, and her neighbor. She taught truth to her children, worked hard, and had creative hands. The woods of the Great Smoky Mountains were a haven — she knew every tree, she respected nature. She had wisdom of the Bible through endless readings. Yet, her 'book learning' in a classroom was minimal, and she wanted more for her children. She was not a complainer, she was content in her world.

Kate Watson Beck and Blanche Watson Blalock remember their mother, Rintha Maples Watson, as a woman who walked in these shoes. 'Aunt Rinthie', as most folks knew her, was married to David Coin Watson in 1899. He died in 1919, leaving her and their seven sons and daughters.

Daughter Ruth was married at the time, and Dicie married soon after. The family, ages 3 1/2 to 19, soon left their farm in the Oldham's Creek community and moved to the Little River logging operations in the Smokies. 'Aunt Rinthie' told her sons if they were moving for work to support her, then she would go along and cook for them.

Blalock and Beck remember the move. They traveled with furniture packed in a wagon which was drawn by their Uncle Noah's two mules, Kate and Beck. 'Girl', their cow, was tied to the back. When the family reached Gatlinburg, 'Ma' and some of the children left the wagon to walk a shortcut through the Sugarlands. At Elkmont the small group forded the river and rejoined their wagon. 'Girl' had never seen anything larger than a creek, and she saw no reason to be on the other side of Little River until 'Ma' went across and coaxed her over with a handful of cornbread.

The Watsons then rode the logging train to Fish Camp where they settled in a company house. They moved from place to place as areas of the Smokies were logged, remaining at the camps until the early 1930s. While there, they also lived at Elkmont, Jakes Creek, Wildcat, String Town (named for the 'string' of houses along both sides of the railroad track), Blow Down (named for the trees that had blown down during an earlier 'cyclone'), and at Tremont near the company store and company hotel.

Arthur and Richard ('Rich') worked as hands on a logging skidder and Bob, only 15, worked as a flagman. Rinthie Watson did washing and ironing for workers and took in boarders. Boarders lived in a 'lobby' that was placed beside the family's company house; the homes and lobbies were moved up and down the tracks on flat cars.

Beck and her sister remembered their mother ordered margarine in 30 pound quantities and stored it in the spring branch to use in her cooking for boarders. It was shipped with small packages of yellow coloring for each pound of margarine.

'Aunt Rinthie' was a woman eager to help neighbors. During the flu epidemic in the teens she cared for two of her own children and assisted neighboring families.

For enjoyment, she had her garden and her 'purties' or flowers. She went to school two short terms where she learned to write only her name. 'Aunt Rinthie' taught herself to read. She read 'The Girl of the Limberlost', 'The Comfort', 'Good Stories', and Zane Gray novels. Blalock remembered her enjoyment from the 'Cubby Bear Stories' in 'The Comfort.' Her mother and a good friend 'Aunt' Maudie Wilson visited regularly to discuss their magazine stories.

'Ma' never seemed lonely. She and neighbors visited and talked of old times, discussed religion, or told tales. 'Aunt Rinthie', a woman of little fear, loved to pass along scary stories.

Beck remembered a time when the family lived in Elkmont near the curve where 'Daddy Bryson' was killed in a train wreck. Neighbors told stories of hearing that wrecked train's whistle late in the evening. These stories had Beck, then a young child, afraid that one evening she would hear the ghostly train sound.

A few years before the Great Depression there was never enough money for more than necessities. 'Ma' found ways of making her home a more pleasant place with pretty creations for crochet patterns and decorative scarves. For a fireplace covering or sham to be used in the summer, she placed leaves and ferns on a white cloth and, with broom straws, sprinkled a mixture of buttermilk and chimney soot over them. When the leaves and ferns were removed there was a gray cloth with white leaf and fern designs.

As her children grew and the two older boys married, 'Aunt Rinthie', Bob, and Kate returned to their Oldham's Creek farm. Blanche moved away to attend Pittman Center High School.

Today, Blalock and Beck are the only remaining of the seven. They cherish memories of their mother, a charitable woman, and some of her ways have become their ways. The two recall her sitting through the night placing onion poultices on a child's chest, and they remember her dancing an Indian rain dance to the delight of her grandchildren. An old Cherokee greeting is recalled: "Sty you or stickie sty you?" (are you stout or not so stout?) - or "how do you do?"

The most special of all these remembrances is the memory of their mother's inner strength, a strength gained by faith and offered for others.

The Funeral Train

One Southern small town had about the same handful of businesses as any other small Southern town in the early 1920s. Sevierville was no exception. There was the blacksmith shop, the mercantile, the bank, and the town undertaker.

The undertaking profession was the one that required a big heart and sympathetic nature. Harold Atchley said his father, the late James Atchley, had both when he opened his furniture and undertaking supply business on Main Street, Sevierville. He was selling coffins and couches from the same store - and so were the Rawlings who were in business before him.

Atchley remembered when there were deaths in small communities during his father's first years. The men with the best horses and wagon would come into town for a coffin while others dug the grave. Neighbor women began cooking for the family. The one or two funeral trains (or marches) on foot that Atchley recalled were a sad, lonely sight with a wagon bearing the casket leading mourners to the grave.

Many had no money for a store-bought coffin when Atchley's father started his business. Some families kept pre-cut pieces of walnut, oak or pine lumber in their barn lofts or chicken houses, in the dry, until the time the pieces were needed for a coffin. After the men built the coffin, the women lined it with soft satin or a silk-type material. Bodies were prepared, if not by the undertaker, by someone in the community.

Death had a more frightful look around the turn of the century. Bodies were dressed in black (unless an infant) and pennies (then later nickels and dimes) were placed over eyelids for keeping them shut. Without make-up or embalming fluid, the faces were as colorless as the material lining the caskets. Perhaps, because of the nighttime tales or because of the more superstitious nature of some people in the early 20s, there was a fearfulness about death that is seldom seen today.

Death brought whole communities together to sit through the night with a saddened family who, then as many today, leaned on the Lord for solace. Atchley said in the summertime there would be a yard full of mourners at a home and in the wintertime, a houseful. The funeral, because there was no embalming, would be held the following day and usually outside by the grave.

When his father was assisting families in the home, Atchley said he would stay the night, too. There was limited transportation and poor roads that prevented him from returning home in the evening. James Atchley was paid five to fifteen dollars for those early services. Factory made caskets, primarily of wood, sold for sixty to ninety dollars.

After training in Knoxville from a friend and in Nashville, Atchley's father received his embalming license in 1928, and became Sevierville's first licensed embalmer. In those early years at Atchley's funeral home the business operated with two horse drawn hearses - one plain and one ornamental with fancy windows and carbon lamps. Even when the Atchley's purchased a T Model Ford, the horse drawn buggies continued to be in use because of the poor condition of area roads.

The T Model and, later, a 1922 or '23 model Chevrolet were rebuilt by a local garage to become funeral coaches, said Atchley. The first manufactured hearse was a 1934 Meteor with a GM chassis. After 8 or so years since opening, Atchley's and Rawlings were serving as the county's ambulance service with their hearses. New-born babies were riding home from Broady's hospital in the same hearse that carried old grandfathers to the graveyard. In the beginning, a cot and a bed pan were the only equipment that transformed the hearse to an ambulance, said Atchley.

By the early 1950s, fewer families had bodies brought to their homes to lie in state. Atchley's seldom used the red drape backdrop and lamps carried to the homes. Folks were now buying artificial flowers for funeral services and paying from two dollars to ten for the largest arrangement at Atchleys. Families continued to bring fresh flowers from their homes before florists began operating in Sevierville.

Since Atchley's father opened his business, Sevier County has not seen deaths in numbers such as those caused by the flu epidemic around 1915 or 1917. James Atchley was almost one of its victims; his illness was so great, family members thought he, too, had died of the flu. Probably, the greatest tragedy in Atchley's father's years of operating his business was when the Pittman Center family was brought to his funeral home in 1938. Six family members and two visitors (who were taken to Newport) drowned in the August election-day flood, said Atchley.

In the very early years, there were many infant deaths - about two a month, recalled the funeral director.

Through the years, since Atchley began helping his father at the age of twelve, working at the funeral home has been his life. Often Atchley has been asked, "How do you get used to death?"

"You don't," he said. You offer sympathy and understanding.

As Atchley's Funeral Home continues to operate not far from their first Main Street location, it is one of the few operations where one generation has learned from the last - from James Atchley to his son, Harold to his two sons Albert and D.J. The family business continues, spanning over 75 years, in a growing small town.

Paddle Your Own Canoe

Oliver Ogle sits in a ladderback rocker keeping warm by the wood stove. Pine knots crackle in the stove, and there's the smell of his chewing tobacco in the small log home in Huskey's Grove, a few miles north of Gatlinburg. The round logs make a solid house that nestles on his hillside land near the Great Smoky Mountains National Park.

Ogle, age ninety as the Twentieth Century winds down, has been a carpenter and landscaper for most of his adult life. He still makes wood carvings and baskets that his daughter, Janavee Ownby, sells in her Gatlinburg shop, Ownby's Woodcrafts.

But today Ogle is taking time to sit and talk with a visitor, reminiscing about his boyhood days at school in the Little Dudley community of the Great Smokies. He recalls walking barefoot to school on a late summer day when he was maybe six or seven. The mountain school was much the same as hundreds of others in Appalachia shortly after the turn of the century.

"Dudley Creek School was a one-room school house - a high school because it sat high on a hill," Ogle says with a twinkling eye. The building was a distinct part of his community, he remembers, with its small white frame of weatherboard planks and its bell encased in a steeple. Nearby were stacks of boards to build a church for Little Dudley; while it was being built, folks held their meetings at the school.

Inside were benches ten to twelve feet long, hewn from hard poplar trees. There was little comfort on a bench of this mold, but comfort was not what young Ogle was there for, he says. He was there to learn from the primers and beyond.

Seated with a coarse paper tablet in his lap, he would place his reader in the book box on the bench in front of him and look around the familiar room, little changed from his previous school term eight months ago. Four large windows on either side of the benches brought in the sun's rays throughout the day and opened the outside woods to the children's daydreaming imagination. Window sticks propped the framed panes and let in a small hint of a breeze to cool the late August heat.

In the back of the room stood a broom and a table with a water bucket. He and the other children enjoyed carrying water, Ogle says, because making the quarter mile trip to the spring and back got them out of class a fair amount of time. Around the room, papers were posted with admonishing remarks like, "Paddle your own canoe" and "Do you know it or only think you do?" Without the students, the room had little color - only a blackboard attached to a wall with no paint. In the front of the room was a pulpit for Sunday church services with a table nearby for the school teacher.

Ogle's teacher, a young Earnest Proffitt, had his hands full, Ogle remembers, because two older girls wanted to court him at the same time. Teachers of the day were not much older than students. Age was relative in the eyes of parents. Ogle recalls a family who recorded the ages of their children a bit older than they were, so they could quit school earlier and stay home to work the farm.

Those who remained in school began their day at Dudley Creek with a recitation of 'The Lord's Prayer." Then came lessons - English, arithmetic, reading, physiology or health, history, geography and spelling. At recess, they played baseball and tag. Lunch was eaten from a basket or a Karo syrup gallon bucket, with peaches and apples from a nearby orchard as extra treats.

The school days stretched into weeks, and the orchards stopped bearing fruit, and the summer heat turned to cold. When the wood stove could no longer provide enough warmth to compensate for the bitter cold walks to school, another school term came to a close. Oliver Ogle would walk the three quarter mile trail home one final time before Christmas and would not return to classes until the end of the next summer. Then he would be back, reciting "The Lord's Prayer," learning his arithmetic and asking himself, 'Do I know it or only think I do?'

This story is a reprinted article from the Knoxville News Sentinel. It is included by permission.

Fruit Basket Upside Down

"A pair of overalls and a dollar a day is good enough for anyone," Martha Graham, born 1918, remembered hearing President Herbert Hoover say during the Great Depression. Whether those living then agreed - such was the way for many of that day.

Life as a teenager in the 1930s was a life of strict discipline, said Graham. Youth showed respect for those older, those in authority or leadership such as the President, parents, or a Sunday School teacher. "Their mouth was the prayer book," she said of her elders.

Graham's teen years were filled with hard work, some play and a lot of church on Sunday - three times a day. Folks made the best of hard times and enjoyed life in spite of them. However, Graham said that she would not wish for anyone to go back and live them over.

Graham's pre-adult life covered much ground. 'No,' she knew of no racism; and 'yes,' she knew a slave - a 90 + year old lady, the sweetest she ever knew. A curfew wasn't necessary when your mother walked along behind you, carrying the lantern as you and your boyfriend walked home from church. This same boyfriend was not allowed to sit with you in church, and he is the one who would be rocked by neighbor boys on his walk back from your house.

And, 'yes,' there was a bully up the road who beat up Graham every day for no reason until she and her cousin 'beat him up.'

There was a brutal murder, she remembered after her teen years, just off the spur at a 'beer joint.'

Discipline kept young school students in tow; they did not throw spitballs, because they were afraid of a whipping from the teacher (one that would raise you off the floor) and a whipping when they returned home.' Nor, did students wish to stand with chewing gum on their nose as punishment, she said.

Graham learned to drive through the Great Smokies during a time when driver's licenses were not required and Fords sometimes pulled better in reverse than going forward.

Young people's parties were daytime parties. Graham's father told, "You choose darkness rather than light, because your deeds are evil." Daytime parties were fun, just the same. Young people played fruit basket upside down (musical chairs) and post office. "We'd get a little sugar all along," Graham said with a laugh.

Not so fun were the times when Graham heated her feet with a rock and then ran off to bed... or when she walked two miles from Mill Creek to Pigeon Forge to sell blackberries for ten cents a gallon. The walk was rewarded, however, by trading berries to Mrs. Mary Henry for piano lessons.

She talked about her mother selling milk for ten cents a gallon and about bathing in a galvanized tub on Saturday night by the fireplace. She told that relatives passed on clothes to be remade for school and church and that she wore sack dresses made from fertilizer sacks for everyday. People, then, slept on straw ticks or those made of hay or leaf bags until in Roosevelt's day there was a government program that provided cotton for making mattresses. The women of Pigeon Forge made them upstairs in Stott's store.

Graham walked behind a plow pulled by the family's horses, Her family, the Franklins, rose early with their mother saying, "Get up, the day's half gone; it's 4:00 (a.m.)," recalled Graham. They worked the fields until lunch and then swam in the river a little while as their mother rested. They shouted as they entered the river, sending skinny dippers scampering up the hill.

Discipline and religion kept weaving its way in and out of Graham's teen years. Once she was punished with two or three doses of castor oil and a whipping - when she and the whole school sneaked out for a long hike on the teacher's birthday. Graham quickly noted that the pranks of the day were not worth the punishment.

She attended her first ten school years at Pigeon Forge and the last two in Gatlinburg. She played basketball in grades five through twelve. At first, she played barefoot and in a dress on an outside court. Later, the team wore uniforms with long knee shorts or bloomers. Graham's father told her she could only play wearing a dress. Her mother convinced him to attend one of the games, and he saw that it was difficult for his daughter to play in a dress. He permitted her to wear the uniform.

She talked of attending games in the back of Walt Benson's cattle truck, seated in chairs with a canopy overhead.

At Pi Beta Phi High School, while staying in the dormitory, Graham met her future husband. Girls in the dorm were only allowed to walk down to the street which was separated from the school yard by a fence. "CCC (Civilian Conservation Corp) boys sat at the fence and flirted with the girls; and we'd flirt with them, and that's how I met my husband." Graham was married in the last of her teen years at nineteen. She borrowed fifty dollars for a complete wedding outfit: a hat, coat, shoes, and dress which she purchased at Wade's Department Store in Sevierville.

By Graham's teen day's standards in the Great Smokies, her family was as well off as most folks, maybe with a little more than some, because her father was a carpenter. Still, she joked and said, "We were so poor, we had to stand on a sack of fertilizer to raise an umbrella."

Could teens of today have survived in Martha Graham's younger days. A once a week bath might be hard to imagine; but, driving without a license... that's a different story.

A Lot of Spunk

The Smoky Mountain Railroad train comes rolling into Sevierville and crosses the trestle over the Little Pigeon. Underneath the rumbling train, a few feet below the trestle, lie two young girls on top of the concrete pillars. Dorothy Trotter (McMahan) and her friend Carol Hatcher have found one more challenge in their everyday adventures at downtown Sevierville.

With a little imagination and a lot of spunk, life in the 1920s and '30s around Cedar Street and beyond in Sevierville is of a different flavor than the life youngsters will know in later years.

Dorothy Trotter is the young daughter of Emert and Ollie Tinsley Trotter; she has four brothers and four sisters. Her father is a big man, the town blacksmith and self taught veterinarian. When a strong man comes to town and puts on a show by lifting one corner of a T Model in front of Park Theater, friends and neighbors coax Trotter to show the man what he can do. He laughs and picks up the entire back end of the Ford. A block or so from her father's blacksmith shop, Dorothy and her friends fill their days in play on Court Street in one direction or around the Methodist Church and down Cedar Street in the other.

After returning from the circus in Knoxville with older brothers and sisters, the young girl and her friends create their own circus shows and carnivals. She performs the death defying acrobatic acts, and, in the end, goes home with a broken bone. Tarzan of the apes imitators swing from trees, and neighborhood children roller skate or hide around the Methodist Church playing whoopie hide or hide and seek.

John Fox, the Worth family, and the younger Rogers children are continually active along Cedar Street. Many times, the boys — and sometimes the girls — play long and hard with periodic fights breaking out. In one fast retreat, Dorothy feels the effects on her back side as an angry David Waters fires BBs at the enemy.

Members of the First United Methodist Church on Cedar Street play a role in young people's lives around town. They hold two and three week long summer Bible schools, plan 'Mystery Mother' banquets and conduct Tom Thumb weddings for those about waist high. (Mothers dress their children in make-believe wedding gowns and suits, and the children play act the ceremony.)

Mrs. Jenny Bailey, looking for an excuse to see a good Western, takes Dorothy along to the Seaton Theater for a Saturday matinee. Nearby, on Park Road (Park Way), folks around Sevierville are enjoying nice lunches at Rose's Tea Room.

For a little more rambunctious fun, the girls decide the boys have taken over the Shepherd swimming hole long enough. Clad in underwear that covers more than outerwear of the future, the girls shout fair warning to any unsuspecting boy skinny-dippers and jump in the water. Soon the swimming hole is for boys and girls, all dressed appropriately in summer underwear.

Everyday is not play day for youngsters in downtown Sevierville; there are chores that must be done. In a family of eleven, everyone pitches in. Brother Mel mops and polishes the floors, and H.D. does the wash because he enjoys running the motor and wringers on the first electric Maytag in the town. Dorothy and her sisters hang the clothes out to dry. John, being one of the oldest, is the gardener and one of the first to work outside the home. He goes out to the Georgia peach truck, that comes to Sevierville every Friday and Saturday, and he buys fruit for canning. The thrifty brother waits until Saturday at noon to buy. He can then pay less for the ripened fruit.

Work increases around holidays. Sister Sadie and Dorothy's mother are the only two allowed in the kitchen. Sadie does the more fancy dishes, the pastries and biscuits, and their mother does the 'plain cooking.' At Thanksgiving and Christmas, there will be ham, home made cranberry sauce, macaroni and cheese instead of potatoes, real fruit salads and lots of desserts. Emert Trotter goes to Arlie McCown's Meat Market ahead of time to buy a live turkey to fatten for the big meal. By the time the bird is big enough to eat, the Trotter children yell and bellow and ask that their new pet be spared... and it is.

At Easter time, Mrs. Trotter boils two dozen eggs for breakfast and some for coloring with food coloring. Seated around the breakfast table, the Trotter children have egg fights (one person pecks another's egg with his own to see which egg will crack first.) A champion egg fighter will emerge with the hardest shelled egg.

Many holidays will pass and Sevierville will grow and change. Dorothy Louise Trotter will later marry M. B. McMahan and the two will rear one son, M.B. McMahan, IV (Beetle).

Spending a lifetime around downtown Sevierville sharpens images of past childhood years in the 1920s and '30s. McMahan, in her seventies today, tells of playing football with the best of the boys and of riding the Clydesdales that her father brought home on weekends from his logging job in the Smokies. The horses were so big, young riders' legs stuck out from either side of the animals' bellies.

McMahan recalls learning to drive when she was eight. Her older brother John was city mail carrier. While he was home for a break and a nap, she slipped his car out and drove down the street. At age twelve, McMahan was riding in her brother's bigger and better cars. His Packard convertible was a big thrill for a young girl.

Probably the biggest thrill, however, for McMahan was when President Franklin D. Roosevelt stopped his driver on his way through Sevierville to the Great Smoky Mountains National Park dedication to recognize two young Sevierville girls. McMahan and her friend Hatcher were outside Hatcher's house, barefoot and in their every-day dresses waiting for a glimpse of the President. As soon as he was in sight, the two jumped up and began screaming and yelling. The President called them to his car and patted them on the head - a kind gesture that would forever remain in their memories.

Parents and adults, those older and not so old, were influences on a young girl's life in those years. There seemed to be a better connection between the young and the old. McMahan recalls having read to an older neighbor - Aunt Emma Caton, who supported herself as a milner until she became blind after becoming a young widow.

From the quieter moments listening to her father talk of his fox hunting dogs, Sing and Tone, to her boisterous 'Tom-boy' days, Dorothy Trotter McMahan had an adventurous young life. Perhaps, McMahan's youthful antics could have labeled her Sevierville's own girl version of Tom Sawyer or Huck Finn.

Ma's Old Timey Ways

Early morning darkness waits for the sunlight to break through the trees with the coming of a new day in the Great Smoky Mountains.

It is 4:00 a.m., and the family is still resting soundly from yesterday's hard work... until the smell of frying side meat and steaming coffee reaches their noses and interrupts their dreams.

Ma dips cold water from the water bucket to the wash pan and washes her face and hands before going out to the spring box. She builds a fire in the wood cook stove as her oldest daughter comes in to help with breakfast. The early riser walks by lantern light to the spring for cold milk and butter - her long dress is dampened by the misty dew.

After breakfast is cleared from the table, the family begins their morning work. Ma helps the girls set out the dish pans and fill them with hot water from the cook stove. They make the beds and sweep the floors.

Outside, Ma listens to the chirping song birds, and her spirits lift. With an apron full of corn and a 'here, chickie, chickie, chickie,' she gives the chickens at her feet their morning feed. A grin crosses her face as she listens to Pa out in the field, talking straight and loud to his stubborn mule who forgot his gee from his haw. Soon, she will get her hoe and join the rest of the family in the field. She'll put the baby on a pallet in the shade with his sister and work until time to take the October beans from the stove to the table.

By dinner time, the clear skies have darkened and Ma has no hopes of finishing in the fields later in the day. Looks as if this will be a good, ground-soaking rain. With trees shading the house and dark clouds overhead, Ma lights the oil lamp and gets a Montgomery Ward catalogue. Today will be right for making that new dress she'd been putting off, so she searches the catalogue pages for pattern ideas. After the newspaper pattern and dress pieces have been carefully cut, Ma sits at the peddle sewing machine and begins her task. She hears a cry of pain from the barn where the children have been with their Pa. A chisel for making puncheons has fallen from a shelf and there's a cut toe.

Ma wipes the tears with her apron and reaches between the

Rosebud and Cloverine salve boxes for the carbolic acid salve on the mantel. She cautiously dresses the cut in clean rags and comforts the child.

At near supper time, Ma puts the dress away to finish another day; she has time to fry potatoes and put on another pan of corn bread. The busy mother is interrupted by a knock at the door. Good news is that a neighbor's baby is much better after a bout with the phthisic. Her heart is glad for the baby's mother, as she recalls when she recently helped to lay out a baby that had died of diphtheria. Ma thanks the neighbor for the news and invites her to stay for supper.

After the dish water is poured in the hog's slop bucket, Ma sits down by her spinning wheel. She'll spin and tell her children stories from her past, and, perhaps, she'll read from "The Beautiful Story" Bible story book. She'll check her starter for some salt rising bread and think about baking tomorrow for Sunday. There's a good fat hen for a nice Sunday dinner, and the pink roses by the porch will make a pretty table bouquet. Perhaps, the family will walk over to her mother's for a visit.

The children's feet are washed, and they are in bed now. Ma sits combing her long dark hair; the clock on the mantel strikes eight. Pa lays down his spectacles and the Bible he's been reading, and the two enjoy the quiet as they reflect with satisfaction on this good day they know 'the Lord hath made.'

In future years, sons and daughters will choose a day to celebrate mothers and they'll remember, with great respect and a tender heart, these women and their old timey ways.

*Talks with Kate Beck, Archie Ray McMahan, and the late Laura Watson, provided the information for this story.

Warm Memories For Cold Days

Sunlight sparkled off the white blanket of snow that surrounded Lavator and Arlie (Arlena) Walker's home at White's community. The deep snowfall had left the big farmhouse barely distinguishable from its surroundings.

Yellow flames flickered in the fireplace and coal oil lamps softened images inside rooms papered with flower patterned building or wall paper. The thick paper and weatherboard were all that separated the cold outside from the wood burning warmth inside. An eight day clock, on the mantel piece that was made by Levator Walker, ticked the moments away through the quiet nights.

In later years in another warmer home, a pretty pieced quilt covered the day bed in the living room of the country home, and handmade furniture that was made in the workshop outside was placed about the room. Levator Walker filled the room with music as he played on his bellows organ or pump organ.

One Walker child, Annie Fae - born 1919, looked through the window panes, watching snow fall, and thought about the walk up the steep hill to the barn that she, her brother and sister would make to feed the chickens each night. They wore brand new overshoes that had been bartered for with peas at the Corner Store in Sevierville. Their mother walked the same path to milk the family's one cow. Annie Fae watched as she squeezed warm squirts of white milk from a patient cow that methodically munched on mouthfuls of hay or sweet feed (ground corn.) The elder Walker could feel the warmth from the cow's belly near her head as she filled the milk bucket one squirt at a time.

The warmth back inside was welcomed and appreciated. In her first home - Annie Fae remembered evenings when the Walker children picked seeds from cotton that was spread across the hearth. The hot fire was too hot on the children's one side and the cold away from the fire was too cold on the other. Still, both Walker houses were better suited for cold temperatures than the house where Annie Fae's father was raised. He told of times when it was so cold the food would freeze on his plate before it was eaten.

Winter days began early at the Walker house as Lavator Walker rose around 4:00 a.m. to build a fire and have breakfast with his family before walking to work at the Sevierville Lumber Company (between present day Co-op and Wendy's). Walker was a carpenter; his workday started at 6:00 a.m. Work had not always been available for Annie Fae's father. He told of a time during the depression when he had walked three or four miles in a deep snow that was above his knees to hang a french door to earn money.

Her father, a kind, calm man, never complained of the cold. As a young man he invited its bitter chill when he and his brother Jim broke through ice covering Gist's Creek and dove in - just for the fun of it. Lavator Walker told that the dive rid him of a toothache.

Another cold winter time, when Annie Fae was only five or so, she remembered being carried by her father to a literary society meeting at the school. From her old house it was about a half a mile in the deep snow; but her father would not miss those periodic speeches and debates with community friends and family.

As the little White's community girl grew older and began to attend school, about a tenth of a mile from her new house, her mother dressed her warmly for the winter days. Active play was warmth enough for the little boys and girls. Soon, Annie Fae would have her wool stockings pushed down and her long underwear scooted up because they were too warm. After school, the Walker children would listen to their father tell stories and their mother read from the Bible or from a book of Grim's Fairy Tales.

At a still later age, the evening winter chores began to include carrying water from the school and the well. They helped their mother do quilting on quilting horses similar to a carpenter's saw horses to earn money. The Walker's were paid a penny a yard (of thread) for their work; if it took five hundred yards of thread to quilt an entire quilt, they were paid five dollars.

There was a time to do winter chores and a time for play in the cold snows for the Walker children. They bundled warmly and spent hours and hours making snow men, sledding on wooden sleds and pasteboard boxes, and tramping through the woods. The children were inside only long enough to thaw red fingers and toes in a pan of cold water and return to the outdoors again. Sometimes their mother would hold her youngsters' toes in her hands to warm them from the cold.

Memories of these winter sights and sounds give joy to Annie Fae Walker Kerr. She now has children, grand- and great grandchildren of her own. She still recalls with clarity the icicles hanging long from the porch roof, buggy tracks in the snow, and soft breezes blowing skifts of snow from the trees - warm memories of cold winter days.

Lavator and Arlie Walker with children:
Frank, Ruby and Annie Fae

Time For The Cows To Come Home

It'll be getting dark soon. Time to go hunt the milk cow.

Marthie and Lindy begin to make their way to the back field where they're sure to find old Bossie grazing to her heart's content.

They crawl between the barbed wire fence and step over creek rocks, the easiest route for the hunt between two steep hillsides. To cross the gap and reach the flats, Marthie and Lindy soon must decide between the long, more distant, cow trail or the short, steep cow trail.

In these hills and hollers, even the cows sometimes have trouble sticking to the side of the near straight up and down trails that look better suited for goats, not cows.

Breathless, the two reach the top by edging up the trail and decide to sit a while. Marthie reaches into her blue jean pocket for a piece of brown paper bag and a match to smoke a roll of rabbit tobacco she gathered along the way. Lindy, the more daring of the two, coaxes her friend to try a dip of sweet snuff that she slipped from her Granny's cupboard. Marthie chooses her rabbit tobacco because she has vivid recollections of Lindy's green face the first time she ever took a dip.

Rested and full of gab, the two girls walk down the back side of the gap and past the mill holler. They feel the hot summer temperature cool down in the thick shade of the trees and from the passing cold creek water. Lindy cups her hands and dips into a chilly spring for a drink of water before the two continue their hunt. Marthie breaks a tiny birch stick off a tree limb to chew on.

The deep and low clanging of a cow bell is heard in the distance. Marthie and Lindy reach the flats and see old Bossie on the other side of the blackberry briers. They walk by a pile of slate rocks, and one cautions the other to stay clear, because, "there's a good place for a nest of copperheads." Careful to miss the fresh cow piles, the two girls walk up behind the family milk cow and head her for home.

They wish their dog, old Ted, hadn't died last year. All their Mama had to do was walk out of the house with her milk bucket and a bucket of bran feed for the cow and Ted was ready to take off and bring the cows home alone.

Back at the milk gaps, the girls lay down the bars for old Bossie to walk through from the fenced-in pastures to the barn. Their Mama is waiting to milk the cow and finish with the evening's jobs.

Bringing the cow home is as much a part of Marthie and Lindy's day as eating a meal, and it will be tomorrow, and the day after, and so on until there's a break when the baby calf comes along.

Older folks know of cow hunting days, days for walking with a cousin or for time alone "out of doors". They know how to enjoy the singing birds, or to stop along the way just to look up at a tall pine and wonder how far into the sky the dark green limbs can reach. They'll remember those days, and at evening time, know it's time for the cows to come home.

This story is for cousins Christine, Sue, Lola, and Lorene.

"Memoirs Of Living In Big Greenbrier"

The following was taken from "Memoirs of Living in Big Green-brier", written by Evolena Ownby (b. 1907 - d. 1983). It is included here by permission of Ownby's brother Estel Ownby and sister Velma Ownby Lamons, and the Smoky Mountain Historical Society.

"Nestled in the heart of the Great Smoky Mountains is a little community called Big Greenbrier. This community, at one time, boasted that it had three general merchandise stores, two churches, one public school, a hotel, three blacksmith shops, five corn mills and approximately 500 people. Big Greenbrier is now a part of the Great Smoky Mountains.

Before Grandmother (Sophia Evans Ownby) died, daddy bought land and built a house on the Upper Cowflat Branch. After her death we moved in the Spring of 1910. To get to this upper area of the stream a great steep bluff had to be climbed.

The house that daddy built had one large room with a lean-to kitchen and a porch all the way across the other side. In the large room we had beds on both sides of the fireplace and in the back of the room. The day we moved I have a faint memory of singing, "Happy Day." I'm sure it wasn't a happy day for mother.

The Cowflat Branch was isolated from the rest of the community. There was a sled road that wound around the mountain for about a mile and a half. It was up hill all the way to the house. We did not have any close neighbors; the hills and valley were all that we could see.

The land was a long narrow valley with large hills on both sides. It was a small beautiful level valley with rich mountain soil. A level area in the steep mountains was valued indeed.

Our yard was a large one. We did not have any grass growing in the yard because we did not have anything with which to keep the grass cut. My sisters kept the yard swept clean. Daddy put a pine paling fence all around the house. He split the pine palings with a froe and sharpened one end... to keep out the chickens and all the other critters. Nothing could get across the fence.

Just below the house was a huge grayback rock. It was almost as high as the house. One could walk on it and we ran and played on it lots of times.

Mother built a hen nest right on top of it. One day, the (settin') hen flew off just as mad as she could be. Mother went to see what was wrong and found a copperhead snake in the nest. She could not get close enough to the snake to kill it with a hoe, so she had some of the older children carry some hot coals of fire from the fireplace (to kill the snake). (Before the snake was killed it threw poison at mother, but she stayed a safe distance).

The first thing that really stands out in my mind (while living here) was the birth of my youngest brother, Estel (1910). I was sleeping on one side of the fireplace, and mother was in bed on the other side. Sometime in the night I woke up and someone told me I had a baby brother.

Grandfather Whaley, mother's father, Dr. Frederick Clark, and Louisa Whaley were there that night. Grandfather (John) Whaley... was called Dudley John. He helped to bring the greater part of the later generation into life in the community. He was called "the baby catcher."

Another of my earliest memories was "My Aunt Charlotte's Bible Story Book," that I called "My Jesus Book." This book played a great part in my young life.

In the two years we lived on Cowflat Branch: Daddy... started an apple and peach orchard, (and he) built a small barn with a corn crib on one side of it. One year he made more corn than he could get in his crib, (so) he boxed up one end of the porch and put his corn in it. He usually kept a horse, two cows, and a hog or two.

It was hard to make a living on that little farm. I don't remember us going hungry. Most of the time we had most of the necessities, but not any luxuries while living there. We had our own meat, grew our vegetables, and had our own milk and butter. Daddy grew cane and made molasses every year...

(Once,) Uncle John Ownby and his wife, Aunt Nellie (Maples) Ownby came and spent the summer with us. He helped daddy and the boys in the field and Aunt Nellie taught my sisters how to make willow baskets.

There was plenty of willow growing down below the house. They got the small switches and peeled the bark off before making the (beautiful) baskets. (Aunt Nellie) would dye her switches with different herbs or barks from the trees.

Mother worked to keep everything clean and taught her family the same. We didn't have store-bought soap all the time; mother made her own. She put her ashes from the fire in a large gum barrel. She kept them there until the barrel was full, (then) she poured water over the ashes in the barrel and let it drip out. It (made) strong lye.

(Mother) kept the fats from the hogs that were killed for meat. She put this lye and fats together and boiled them until it was thick enough for soap. It was a strong soap, and (it was good for cleaning clothes).

She used the old time scrub board and boiled the white clothes, and she scrubbed the colored clothes and took her battling stick to loosen the dirt in them. Everybody had a battlng stick and a battling board. It usually took a whole day to do the washing and... a day to do the ironing. We had the old time heating irons. We either heated them in front of the open fire in the fireplace or on the cook stove.

Money with which to buy clothes was scarce. Mother made (for) me two dresses out of some woolen scraps that came from Arthur Cantrell's store in Emerts Cove. She could take anything and make something nice out of it.

Mother... would knit wool socks for the whole family. Daddy bought the wool, and we cleaned it. Mother carded it into small rolls and spun it into thread on the spinning wheel. In the Fall when we would first start wearing (the wool socks) they would stick and scratch my legs...

In the summer of 1912, Daddy came home one day and said, "We are going to move off the Cowflat Branch." There were no tears shed over moving. Daddy swapped his place... to the James Whaley family for his place on the right hand fork of the little Pigeon River (across from the Ownby Cemetery).

Because of bad transportation the two families swapped everything they could in the way of furniture. We had to haul everything we could move in a sled around a mountain road. At the main road it was picked up in a wagon and taken to our new home.

You may talk about Daniel Boone and David Crockett living in the wilderness. The Sam Ownby family almost went into a wilderness when they moved to the Cowflat Branch, and (then) it seemed we were almost going into another one."

NOTE: Evolena Ownby later taught school until she was in her sixties. She never grew past forty-seven inches in height, but she never let her size stop her from achieving her goals in life.

As her senior years approached, she wrote, "My life has been a happy one. I have had to do a lot of pushing, but I guess everyone who has a real happy life has to do a lot of it. It takes pushing, grit and the grace of God to have a success in life."

"A Hill To Climb"

Reva Manning sits in the kitchen of her old 1800s white farm house in the Sims Chapel community. Her arthritic hands are no longer busy in the summer garden, milking the cows or filling orders in her country store. Though her hands are still and her walk is supported with a cane, her wit is sharp, and she is a joy to those around her.

Her memories are filled with practical recitations - wise and thought provoking for any generation.

Manning's gray hair surrounds a tiny face that lights up as she recites childhood poetry, an old Tennessee song, or pieces from a church program. "There is so much good in the worst of us; and so much bad in the best of us, that it ill becomes any of us to talk about the rest of us." Manning recites, accenting the proper words so that one can imagine her as a school girl standing before class.

She spent her childhood years in the Parrott's Chapel community of Jefferson County in a log home that sits covered with the waters of Douglas Lake. The old Parrott's Chapel Methodist Church still stands, hollow of its furnishings and its congregation who moved to make way for the TVA lake. Beside the church is a cemetery where piney roses bloom each year decorating Manning family member graves.

Nearby is the old Parrott's Chapel school site where shady trees, lakeside homes, and still waters provide a different scene than in the years of Manning's school days.

She remembers those days when her teacher punished students by having them stand on one foot. And, she recalls a teacher who told the children if they wished to be excused, just lay their books on a shelf. All the books were stacked, and the children went outside to play. As they returned later in the day, the teacher waited by the door and switched each one with one swarp. "That was one year, I just as well as not went," said Manning with a laugh.

The old school desks held two students each, and they had hinged lids covering the books and pencils underneath. Manning sat with cousin Ada, as they learned in the one room, one teacher school. There were no free books, free bus rides or free lunches in Manning's high school days. She began to attend a high school in Dandridge, and she remembers some days when she had no money for even a nickel sandwich, so she would do without.

Discouraged by the sometimes muddy walk to catch the bus and the little money for school, Manning said she quit, but not without some effort by teachers coaxing her to return.

Manning was raised through her older childhood years by her father Albert Alfred Manning (a different set of Mannings than her husband), with the help of Aunt Mag (Margaret Jane). Her mother died in childbirth when Reva Manning was eleven. Manning's soft heart shows through the tears in her eyes as she remembers her mother's last days.

Her mother, Dicie Russell Manning, had twins, a boy and girl. The son, Lillard, lived and the baby girl, Lillian, died. The mother was told she would not live, so she called her children to her bedside and told them the sad news. "She asked us to be good and meet her in Heaven," remembers Manning.

About nine years later, before Manning's twentieth birthday, she married Henry Manning. The two rented a home in the area and later settled in their own home. Henry Manning started working for about 75 cents a day farming; but, most of his life, he and his wife operated Manning's grocery, first in Jefferson County, then in a small building near the house where Reva Manning lives today (Henry died in 1987.)

Near the store sits an old yellow gas pump and a school bus, driven by Henry Manning around the 1950s and '60s. Manning remembers the stacks of feed bags, RC Colas and moon pies and her children sneaking in for cigarettes. A typical country store, it was the gathering place for the community, for men to talk politics and to whittle, and for passing out free ice cold watermelon slices when a neighbor came by.

Customers came in, took the butcher knife, sliced off a piece of bologna, and said, "I've got a nickel's worth," or a dime's worth," Manning says.

She remembers her husband used his store as a gathering place for neighbors to sign a petition asking the county for a new road through Sims Chapel. He offered free pecans to those who would come out and discuss the petition.

Henry Manning's Grocery is a memory now, the same as the days of driving in her mother's turkeys at night so the foxes couldn't catch them. Reva Manning's parts in the Ghost of Christmas Past and Christmas Present, in the church play, are silent.

These are good memories coming from an intelligent seventy-nine year old (in the 1990's)... one who still recites, "There's a hill that we all must climb. It is called the hill of learning; and if we ever reach the top, there should be no backward turning. Folks should begin to make the start when young like me (she says and grins), and never stop 'till they've gone to school for years and years, and got up somewhere near the top."

And... "Two eyes and two ears and only one mouth have we. The reason I think is clear. It teaches my child that it will not do to talk about all that you see and hear."

And, this one, she recites the same today as she did several years ago in her classroom...

Autumn

"Come little leaf," said the wind one day.
"Come over the meadow with me and play."
"Put on your dresses of red and gold."
"Summer is gone and the days grow cold."

Soon as the leaves heard the wind's loud call,
Down they came fluttering one and all.
Over the brown fields they danced and flew
Singing the soft little songs they knew.

"Crickets good bye, we've been friends so long,
Now the brooks will sing their farewell song,
Saying they're sorry to see us go,
But winter will come and bring the snow."

Soon fast asleep in their cozy beds.
Snowbirds laid a blanket over their heads.
McGuffy's Reader

Reva Manning, the little girl with the parasol, and family:
Grandma Jane, Father Albert and Mother Dicie, and Earl, Leon,
Ralph and Robert, her brothers.

Roamin' After The Roamin' Man

Harvey Oakley, born 1918, had some busy feet to follow if he kept pace with his father, Wiley Oakley, the "roamin' man of the mountains." Wiley Oakley, said his son, was a guide, hunter, fisherman and philosopher, and the father of twelve.

As a boy, Harvey Oakley had plenty of his own roaming adventures with the Great Smoky Mountains and the small settlement of early Gatlinburg for a big backyard.

Smoky Mountain boys were encouraged to get out away from the house, to roam the hills, and not to sit idle inside. As a baby, however, roaming proved difficult for Oakley. (Boy babies wore dresses into their toddler years in the early 1900's.) "Mother put a dress on me, and when she was busy working in the house, she would raise up the bed post and set it down on my dress tail. That way, I stayed put and couldn't go anywhere," remembered Oakley.

That dress kept getting in the way... It caught on a stump when he was playing leapfrog. And it got him caught when it hooked over a nail as he was trying to crawl between the upstairs floor and the downstairs ceiling to find the Christmas candy.

As a very small boy, during a visit to his Granny Lucinda Bradley Ogle's house, Ogle told his Granny he wanted a fried egg for breakfast. "She was cooking in the fireplace, so she opened a shutter on the window (where, outside) there was a hen nest in a wooden Arm and Hammer baking soda box. She got an egg out of the nest... and popped it in the pan for me," he recalled. Had Oakley wanted fried apples instead of eggs, his Granny would have taken up the puncheons in front of the fireplace and reached for them under the floor.

Another of Oakley's adventures was after his family moved from the foot of Mt. LeConte. The house to where he moved was believed to be 'hainted' or haunted, because a man had been killed there. Oakley's father could not be concerned with that, though — he had to put a roof over his children's heads.

Oakley and his brother saw and heard the 'haint' that first night there. "We had to sleep upstairs... As we were lying in the bed, we saw something white-looking going swish, swish up the wall. We bounded out of bed and ran downstairs to Mom and Dad's room where we slept (on pallets) on the floor," said Oakley. The next night, the two Oakley boys did not dare to sleep. Again, the swish, swish; Oakley's brother lit a match and there in the attic were two big white rats (or 'haints'), probably from the mill across the street, carrying old rags to their nest.

Inside that old mill was an abandoned coffin-making shop and a place for making more boyhood adventures. "I remember us kids playing there among the coffins. We played like we were having funerals," Oakley said. Once, they took some of the coffins out to the river to use as boats, then when high waters washed the empty 'boats' downstream, some folks in Pigeon Forge thought a graveyard had been washed away.

The Oakley's later lived across the road from the 'hainted house', on the banks of the Little Pigeon River. "I remember getting my Mother's two wash tubs. I would sit in one and put my feet in the other one and (ride) the rapids down the river," said Oakley. "One day, I saw a water snake in the river that looked like it had wings. I thought I had found a flying snake," said Oakley. With help, Oakley put the snake in a tub and discovered that it had tried to swallow a fish," he said. "So, there went my flying snake."

Harvey Oakley attended Pi Beta Phi school. On one return trip to the school after lunch, he and a neighbor Ogle boy found three gallons of paint. An argument followed over which color each boy wanted for his own. "He got mad, and capped a gallon of paint over my head, and then I capped a gallon over his head," remembered Oakley. After Oakley walked home streaming with wet paint, his sisters washed his clothes in gasoline in the river. "An old boy was fishing below us, and the gas was washing down the river. He struck a match to see if it would burn, and the fire burned up the river and caught my pants on fire," he said.

In recalling his roaming years, Harvey Oakley tells of his brother shooting at a copperhead snake when it poked its head through the boards in the kitchen floor. And, he was never far away from the black bears; they ran cows from the field to the barn at the Oakley home on 'Painter' (panther) Branch.

Perhaps, the greatest moment for young Oakley was when President Franklin D. Roosevelt came to the area for the Great Smoky Mountains National Park dedication. Oakley was so close that he could have touched the President - if not for the secret service.

As Oakley grew, his adventures soon turned from boyhood pranks to a serviceman's adventures in war time and then to the more settled life of a father. Today, he is married to wife, Melba, and they have three married daughters: Sharon, Barbara and Anita.

The ways of this young mountain boy roamin' around Gatlinburg in the twenties have faded into the hillsides.

Harvey Oakley, 1930s

Little River Train Wreck

The morning sunlight was just beginning to break over the mountaintops and erase night's darkness as Oliver Gilland prepared for the train run up from Tremont in the Great Smoky Mountains. His long billed railroad cap and the large handkerchief around his neck would protect his eyes and keep cinders from falling down his shirt collar as he shoveled coal into the blazing boiler.

Gilland left his Tremont lumber company house the same as many times before and walked to engine number nine to wet down the coal before his work day began. The water prevented coal dust from blackening this Little River Lumber Company railroad fireman.

The night watchman had filled the coal tendors in train engines number nine and number eleven the night before. The seven or eight tons of black rock for each engine usually made one day's run. With the train 'coaled up' and the fires kept burning, two of Little River's three engines were ready.

On this Saturday morning in 1929 at about 6:00, numbers nine and eleven slowly crept up the mountainside keeping Gilland and number eleven's fireman Arthur Watson puffing like the engines to keep enough coal for the hard climb.

Engineers Shirley Brooms and Arlie Maples were at the throttles of these powerful black machines. Maples was known to his friends as 'Brownie' because of his love for Brown Mule chewing tobacco. It was said, as he climbed the steep mountain grades he chewed his tobacco to the rhythm of the train's shh, shh, shh; then, as it topped out he spit the tobacco juice across forty cross ties in front of the engine.

The two engineers' locomotives pushed four flat cars each to the head of Marks Creek, between Tremont and Lynn Camp to be loaded with logs.

With five ten-hour workdays behind them, the men may have hoped to return home a little early this Saturday. For the first time Gilland knew of, the workers were bringing out eight flat cars loaded with logs. A normal run was four or five cars.

All cars were loaded and both engines were out in front. A loader on the ninth car was being secured to be left at the loading site. Gilland said he and another worker had gone to the spring to carry fresh drinking water when they witnessed the happenings of the moments ahead.

Workers were tightening chains on either side of the log loader to secure it on a flat car. Both engineers were outside the two engines when (according to a 1977 Knoxville Journal article by Vic Weals) the jolt of the eight loaded cars against the engine started number nine and the flat cars on their fateful journey. This was after the brakes had been eased off to take the slack out of the link that anchored the log loader.

Number nine, with its load, ran into number eleven ten or fifteen feet down the track. The stationery locomotive was no match for the power of the runaway train. The whole lot traveled about a tenth of a mile passing by the few houses on either side of the track at Marks Creek before heading into a sharp curve and jumping the track.

There, just below Ramer Brackins' home, the two mighty engines and their loaded cars ended up in a big hollow beside the track, a mangled mess of iron and steel.

Gilland and some of the railroad workers, after each giving eyewitness accounts of that Saturday train wreck, were 'let go' for a year from the Little River Lumber Company. Arthur Maples had said his father quit after being falsely accused of being at fault in the wreck.

In the Journal article, Arlie Maples said if he had been in the cab when the train started rolling, he could have done nothing more to stop it than he did when he climbed back aboard. The grade was too steep.

Second-hand engines were purchased somewhere in North Carolina, and the lumber company resumed operations. The boiler from number eleven was all that was of any use; it was sent to a Townsend school to be used as a heater. After a year, the railroad workers were allowed back in the company. Gilland, who had been a relief engineer on occasions, went back and drove the passenger train, number 110, from Townsend to Walland. Maples never returned, but his son said he did receive a letter stating new evidence cleared him of blame and asked his forgiveness.

Gilland had only been married a short time to Leafie Dunn when the accident occurred. The young man of twenty or so had started work at Little River when he was about ten years old - carrying water for foreman Bill Franklin's sections crew (the men who maintained the train tracks). He earned one dollar and fifty cents for a ten hour day. He later earned the same pay carrying coal for the steam shovel that was used in making new roads.

By the time Gilland left Little River in 1939, he was making forty-five cents an hour as a train engineer. He took a cut in pay to thirty cents an hour and went to work for the Aluminum Company of America, knowing the lumber work in the Smokies was coming to an end.

As he reflects on his jobs around the Little River trains, Gilland thinks of wiping the big black engines, and he remembers the boiler fire being so hot that he had to shake his overall pant legs to cool them down after stepping up to shovel the coal inside. He was told the fire created two hundred pounds of steam to the square inch.

Gilland knew of the train wreck that killed 'Daddy Bryson,' a Little River train legend; and he tells about how his Grandfather William Ownby walked away unharmed after landing in the river on a runaway caboose.

In spite of the six — and sometimes seven day — work weeks and the ten hours with the trains, and in spite of the cinders, the black dust, the heat, and the heavy scoops of coal, Gilland enjoyed his work at Little River. "It was all we knew," he concluded.

The Little Engine That Did

Folks were probably sitting on their front porch swishing around the lemons in a cold glass of lemonade and fanning with a paper fan from the funeral home as they watched the hacks pull up to the train station.

Sevierville's pace was much slower in the early 1900's - one that moved perhaps at the same rate as the Knoxville, Sevierville and Eastern Railroad or the "Knoxville Slow and Easy". Sevierville residents talk of their memories of the town's railroad days.

When Joy Street's John Fox was a boy, his dad managed the Henderson Springs spa or resort. That resort offered its guests hack service from the train station in Sevierville to the resort near Pigeon Forge. Fox said his father was also an area merchant in those days. The two would climb aboard the passenger car and ride on the wooden benches; cinders flew in from the open windows that 'would beat you to pieces,' he said. They were off to Knoxville where Fox's dad would purchase wholesale goods at Central Avenue and Vine.

The train pulled into a station along the water behind the present day Neyland Stadium, said Fox. He got off and walked to the Southern station where he could see the larger engines come steaming into Knoxville.

Fox talks about a train stop over by Boyd's Creek that was known as Revilo (that is Oliver spelled backwards - Oliver was the engineer who built the railroad, according to John Waters). And Fox remembers the small soft drink manufacturing place in Pigeon Forge that shipped its bottles by train. He tells of how he and others boarded the train for a few cents - ten or so, and carried along their berry picking buckets. When the train jumped the track, the boys hopped off and picked blackberries to carry home to their mothers.

Trains were a fascination to Fox from his youth on. As rail workers loaded and unloaded the large and small crates onto the freight cars, his young mind pondered on what, exactly, could be in all those boxes going to other places. Too, it was something to do for a young boy in a small town, to watch the people boarding and leaving on the K S & E.

When Jimmie Temple, of Temple's Feed and Seed Store, was in his early youth, he recalls that the railroad section crew stored their small dinkey or pump car at the Temple family's Oak City Mills, Chair and Store Company. After the Temples moved to down town, it was exciting for a young boy to see the train pull up in front of his father's store and watch the freight being unloaded, said Temple.

He remembers that loggers from all across the county would bring trucks to haul hay from the train box cars. They bought the western hay from Nebraska and other parts, and from Canada; it was much better for the big teams of horses used in Smoky Mountain logging, he said. The hay was in three wire bales, one hundred and thirty or forty pounds per bale, and it was 'number one' hay.

Temple's father kept a box car or two of the western grain by the store from Friday through Sunday. If it was not all unloaded by the time the train arrived on Monday, a toll was charged for keeping the box car an extra day. Folks such as Frank Roark and his father and Charlie Manis came for the hay. Charlie Blalock's father bought hay from the Temples, and the store hands hauled it out to both Curtis McCarter's riding stables and Clabo's stables on Roaring Fork.

Newspaper articles in Temple's scrapbook reveal further information about the railroad operating in Sevier County. In 1950, according to a January 1974 'Sevier County News Record' article by Claire Hall, the City of Sevierville charged the Smoky Mountain Railroad with not keeping their promise of maintaining the railroad tracks and the streets adjoining. A track ran right through the middle of Bruce Street which the city had paved over in an effort to keep the train off its down town pavement.

One Sevierville City spokesman defended the city by saying businesses on the far end of the tracks were now using trucks for delivery.

A Knoxville Journal photo caption read, "Fireman Calvin Pryor and conductor A.P. Linebarger rest as a road crew digs up a tar compound from Smoky Mountain Railroad tracks down the middle of Bruce Street in Sevierville yesterday."

The Journal article by Chester Campbell on March 14, stated that the street was lined with hecklers as the locomotive inched its way down three blocks after the pavement was dug up. Both the News Record and Journal told how city officials poured oil on the tracks or the front of the train to prevent it from moving along the tracks. Rail workers poured sand over the oil, and the train began to move.

"The little mountain-climbing engine steamed and puffed, jerking back and forth from about 10 a.m. to 1 p.m. before it was able to deliver its three cars to the end of the line, one half mile from where the tar was first encountered," wrote Campbell.

It wasn't too many more years before that little engine puffed its way to the end of the line one last time as stock holders gave in to the reality that the train's business could no longer support its runs from Sevierville to Knoxville. The K S & E or the Smoky Mountain Railroad gave Sevierville its place in the history of days when rail was the primary source of transportation — between the horse and buggy and the automobile. Sevierville, then, could boast its own rail system.

Finding A True Love

Leona Southard was on her way to piano lessons when she found herself in a fix. Her buggy was stuck in the mud until a kind, Southerner happened along and offered a hand.

The young fourteen year old girl did not recognize Perman Franklin as one whose family rented farm land from her father, a prominent Seltice, Washington landowner. Neither did Franklin know it was his landlord's daughter in the buggy. He was too stricken by the thick, wavy, dark hair and the round, soft brown eyes. It was this chance meeting that paired these two for the first time, beginning a friendship and a long storybook romance.

The Bill Franklin family, of the Banner community in the Great Smoky Mountains area, had traveled West after hearing that 'there was a good living to made there.' Far across the plains and into Washington state they traveled, said their Great Granddaughter Ersa Rhea Smith.

Perman's family remained in Washington three or four years until the Smokies called them home again in 1910. In this short time he and Leona became acquainted and a courtship began. Before returning home, Perman's heart was absolutely broken, said Smith, because young Leona broke off their acquaintanceship. Leona, the eldest child, was a carbon copy of her mother who died when she was three. Her father had hopes for college in his daughter's future, and perhaps felt she was too young for a serious courtship.

Back East, Perman's mother, in frail health, confided in her son, "Now son, I don't want you to marry until after I'm gone, and when you do marry, I want you to marry my little Loanie girl." After her death in 1913, correspondence was rekindled by a sympathy card from Leona. Perman was seeing someone else at the time.

He decided to write Leona, and if he received an answer (even though she might never marry him) he would never marry another, Smith said. The courtship, through about 200 exchanged love letters, began and lasted for two years. Leona wrote of plans to attend a college in Chicago, then teach kindergartners. Smith said her grandfather or 'papa' wrote, "Wouldn't you rather have your own children to teach?" His words touched her heart.

Both were dedicated workers in their Sunday Schools and churches.

Perman, one founder of the Pigeon Forge First Baptist, later wrote, "I'll ask you, do you love your Sunday School class? There were over thirty little children at one of the Sunday School classes here - Sunday before last - without a teacher, and finally the superintendent had to appoint a man to teach them."

"When I read of the thirty little children without a Sunday School teacher," wrote Leona on May 12, 1913, "I thought, 'there they will have a place for me, and the sooner the better. Oh, how I love little children.'" Her yearning to come to the East was clear.

The two planned, across the miles, the building of their new home in the Smokies. As Perman, his father and his brother Wiley worked to build their new home, he imagined what life would soon be like with a wife and family. Nestled at the foot of Sugar Camp to catch cool cross breezes and near the meandering Mill Creek, Franklin soon completed his home and barn as he waited for Leona's father to give his consent.

Family and community members knew nothing of his secret love out west, so one presumptuous lady suggested to an embarrassed Franklin, that here was his house; she had the furniture to fill it - so, "how about it?"

In December of 1914, an excited Leona received her engagement ring in time for her 21st birthday. By April of 1915, Perman boarded a train to Spokane where Leona was visiting her maternal grandparents before moving east. She was seated in the window of her grandparent's home when this man she had grown to love, through words on paper, appeared across the street. Leona rushed out the door, across the street and into his arms, said Smith.

As their marriage together began, the two began living out commitments made in letters. She would read to him in the evenings the way his mother did when he was young. He would surprise her with little gifts... a wild flower placed in her hair, a bag of candy from the Saturday visit to town, or a nice handkerchief folded in the shape of a tiny wild animal. At the center of their commitment to each other was their commitment to the Lord, said Smith. With that commitment came a strong faith. "Nanny had such trust, she knew that whatever happened to her could not happen to her without coming through the Lord first," she added.

She surely must have drawn strength from these words only a few months into her marriage when Perman became ill with typhoid fever. With their first child coming, Leona said she had decided that if her new husband died, she would remain in the home he had made for her, Smith retold. The couple survived that early hardship and many others. They worked together, raised four daughters (Lee

Walker, Perna Noland, Iva Campbell, and Rue VanMiddlesworth) and grieved over an infant son's death at only nine days old.

Through their 59 years together, Perman continued to court his wife. As he had written before they were married, 'since I can't do my courting before we get married, I'll have to do my courting after." Their life together, which ended when he died on December 9, 1974, (she died in April of '91), was as they had planned it to be, said Smith. As he brought little gifts, she returned his kindness with a big hug and a kiss with surprise and thankfulness in her voice as if this was the first ever such gift. She continued bringing her husband's favorite evening dessert out on the porch. As years passed, these evenings began to include children, then grandchildren. The youngsters would brush their grandmother's hair, and Papa would sit and watch Nannie with the same admiration shown the young bride from the west.

Smith can hardly speak the words as she describes her Grandparents' love story. She reflects, "My grandparents had a true respect and appreciation for each other. Decade after decade, the family witnessed Papa's courtship of Nannie. He was true to his word; he courted her all the years of their marriage."

Leona Southard

Perman Franklin

The Old Spring Cleanin'

When folks here in earlier years heard the sizzle of hot bacon grease being poured over fresh green lettuce leaves and when it was time to empty the straw bed ticks - they knew spring had arrived in the Smokies.

Blanche Geneva Roberts Ogle, born on Christmas day of 1912, recalls those early spring years as a time when the blackberries were blooming and cleaning and planting times were here.

Her family - her father: West Roberts, mother: Pearl Sutton Roberts, and two brothers lived in the Roberts community which is known today as Jay Ell. Ogle talks of how her father got out early in the season and began burning lettuce and tomato beds. He raked the beds, planted the tiny seeds, and covered them with canvas; then, it was only a matter of time before her mother was killing the lettuce with a mixture of hot bacon grease and vinegar.

In the morning before her father began his day's work, he heated a half cup of water and drank warm water with a little sugar in it (instead of coffee). "I tried it, and it didn't go down so good," said Ogle as she tilted her head back and chuckled in her own distinct laugh.

"My Daddy didn't drink, he never drank a cup of coffee, smoked a cigarette or cursed," she recalls.

For Roberts, there was no time or purpose for vices as he toiled to make a living. It took long hours of spring planting - using most available ground for the gardens to supply almost all winter food. If there was more than enough for the Roberts family, Ogle's dad gave the extra to neighbors. Most neighbors were helpful in that way, remembered Ogle.

In spring time, folks welcomed the fresh warm outdoors after winter's cold. Homes and church doors stood wide open for the bright warm sunshine. At Roberts Methodist Church the voice of Ogle's father could be heard coming through the opened doors as he led the congregation in song. "He could sing, and I couldn't carry a tune in a tow sack," said Ogle.

Perhaps the freshness of the outdoors was a contrast to homes that had been closed to winter cold, making indoor spring cleaning all the more important.

The tiny framed woman of eighty-two (in 1995) looks too small to know of hard work. But, like most younger women of the Smokies in earlier times, she learned hard work from her mother and grandmothers. Spring cleaning taught lessons she still remembers. Ogle, with a smile and warm welcome for everyone, recalls not only the work involved, but the happy times shared while working and playing.

"Mama would take one room and she'd clean two days on that room," remembers Ogle. The women began by cleaning the three fireplaces with two shovels, a broom, and a bucket. With that messy job completed, Pearl Roberts placed a flower patterned curtain over the opening of each fireplace to prevent any remaining soot from coming out into the rooms.

Wood floors were scrubbed with a broom using sand carried in a galvanized bucket from the river. It was a chore to remove all the sand once the scrubbing was done, said Ogle. Each window in the Roberts home had twelve small panes. Ogle recalls the washing with vinegar and water and a little soap. "We'd get a rag, and away we'd go," she said.

Making beds in earlier years was no easy task. Ogle tells that some of the beds they made had a tick filled with straw for the bottom mattress and one filled with feathers on the top. To make the mattresses more comfortable for the next night's sleep, every day the straw was stirred by hand and her mother beat the feather mattress with a broom. Before placing a sheet on the bed, Pearl Roberts had the feather mattress smooth and flat. Ogle's grandmother had seven beds to make each day, and she too had the smoothing technique down to an art. Ogle recalls having asked her grandmother if she could try the broom, but every time she smoothed one lump, another one appeared. In the spring and fall, women emptied the straw ticks. "We'd dump the straw and wash the ticks and head to the big straw stack (to fill them up again,)" Ogle said. "I thought - 'I'll never marry if I have to do all this,'" Ogle remembers.

She did, however, and she and her husband, Mayford Ogle, raised eight children of their own. Today, her grandchildren say that she did, indeed, 'do all this,' as they speak of her continued enthusiasm for spring cleanings.

From the time Ogle was young, she was eager to learn from her mother and grandmothers. Her eagerness for keeping her home went well past spring cleanings. It carried over to her family and her community. "I never did have fine things. The fine things are not the things that matter to me. I love my home and my family," said Ogle.

Blanche Ogle died in late 1997. Her love and influence lives on in family and friends.

Blanche Roberts Ogle

Pearl Roberts

Radar Eyes

When September second rolls around, David Huskey is more-than-likely sitting in the shade by his Douglas Lake cabin working with a bushel basket full of grapes. The outdoor sounds around him are those of katy-dids, the low hum of a passing fisherman's boat, or birds in the trees.

More than fifty years ago on September second, 1945, Huskey was aboard the *USS Mississippi* in Tokyo Bay surrounded by many Allied ships with planes flying so thick overhead that servicemen could hardly see the sky above. The forces were present for the signing of the formal surrender documents by the Japanese Premier and military leaders that ended World War II.

The day of the signing was a solemn time for sailors aboard the battleship, unlike the day of the broadcast announcing Japanese acceptance of Allied Peace terms a couple of weeks earlier. Then, was a time of celebration, Huskey remembered, with fireworks filling the night skies in a show probably unmatched since.

Huskey, at the young age of twenty, had seen his portion of the war as he performed the duties of a fire controlman, third class petty officer, on board the *Mississippi*. He had boarded the ship in late 1943, a short eight weeks after basic training in San Diego, California, and would continue that ship's duty until the close of the war. Huskey said that he joined the Navy rather than the Army because ground fighters ran the risk of coming home injured. In the Navy, he figured he would die or come home whole, and he liked those odds better.

Even though Huskey knew many of the dangers a battleship crew faced, he said being young kept him from worrying too much. He said he thought, "If I'm a goner, I'm a goner; it's not up to me."

While sailors didn't sit around worrying about their circumstances, Huskey said he did not want his words to sound as though war did not affect those in battle. It did. Yet, every minute of the day there were jobs to be done.

He told of an incident during his first year at sea. There was a fire in Turret II where some of the ships 14" guns were being loaded. Huskey said he and others were eating when the dead were carried through - there were forty-two fatalities. They had to continue eating and get back to their duties because the ship was in the midst of bombarding Makin Island at the time.

As Huskey talked of the effects of the World War, he recalled one battle that made its deep impression. Soldiers had backed the Japanese into a large canyon, yet they would not surrender - after repeated warnings. The *USS Mississippi* was called in to destroy them. From aboard ship, many times sailors did not see close-up the destruction of their weapons. This time, however, a marine came on board after the battle to visit his brother, and he told of the demolition, of the men, women, and children he had seen. He described it as the most sickening thing he had ever witnessed.

In a "War History of the United States Ship Mississippi - 1945," carried home by Huskey, battles were briefly chronicled. While he served, according to the history, the ship knocked out all guns on the 'now famous' Bloody Nose Ridge after three days and nights of continual firing at point blank range and after covering the landing with call fire from the twelfth through the nineteenth of September, 1944.

The history continues... the *USS Mississippi* was the flagship of the battleline in Leyte Gulf later that year. Crew members were there twenty-nine days and suffered thirty-eight aerial attacks and one major sea engagement. The first enemy hit came to Huskey's ship in January of '45 when, the history states, "a kamikaze came in low over the water and out of the sun, hitting portside of foremast structure and crashing on the boat deck." This hit resulted in twenty-seven fatalities and damage to the ship's structure, the history stated.

The ship's second wound stripe came as a result of a second kamikaze that hit on the quarterdeck and killed one officer and wounded several others.

Huskey talked of another major encounter that left the ship with burned out rifles, exhausted sailors and brought one more victory toward the end of the War. He told how, in any battle, in any war, it takes everyone working together (including the support from home) to reach a victory... all deserve the credit, he said. Yet, various divisions, generals, tide turning battles came away with records to their credit. The *Mississippi*, according to the history, then held a record when "turret II expended more than one million pounds of ammunition at Okinawa - the greatest amount ever fired by a single turret in any engagement."

The ship was called to battle at Okinawa for the destruction of "the strongest single enemy fortification (Shuri Castle) yet encountered in the Pacific," the history read. Shuri Castle was a 1853 castle that had been modernized to a Twentieth Century super fortification; it had a thirty foot high wall that was six feet thick with a moat surrounding it. The Japanese believed it to be indestructible, and a U.S. ranking former prisoner of war said, "you may take Okinawa, but you'll never take Shuri Castle."

Already, one battleship failed when the ship's ammunition ricocheted off the wall - with direct hits. Aerial bombs had not succeeded. This engagement was counting on the *Mississippi*. "Army and Marine lines had pushed as far south as the Japanese main hope of defense - the Shuri line," the history recorded. With visibility practically nil, the ship launched an observance plane that was unable to get under cloud cover; so, they fired on an invisible target by figuring out the ship's position. *USS Mississippi* history stated, "At 0718 the right gun of turret I belched forth a plume of orange flame and smoke that faded into the mist, and the first of more than a half a million pounds of steel was on its way to Shuri Castle."

The firing was on target. The entire ship's crew were manning battle stations. Huskey was in the control room receiving messages of hits and recording them on a board for the director at the gun controls. On the third day of firing, the weather cleared and the ship moved to within small calibre gun range from shore. The Captain was reminded that only a few days earlier an American ship sank from hits at that range. His determination and the crew's untiring rain of fire power broke through what the Japanese said could not be penetrated, and the castle was destroyed.

After combat repairs, the ship assisted in supporting landings of Allied occupation forces on Japan in August; and by September the second, they and many other battle worn ships were crowded in Tokyo Bay for the signing of surrender terms. Huskey's stint in the Navy was winding down after participating in most of the dozen war operations in what the ship's history called the 'misty Aleutians, the sun-baked Solomons and the typhoon filled China Sea.'

Huskey relives those days with great clarity as Japanese surrender anniversaries pass each year. He speaks of solemn times, of destructive times. He tells how, if he had not been late for chow line, he would have been on deck when one of the two Kamikazes hit his ship. Yet, he can also recall the lighter sides of Navy life.

The former sailor laughs as he speaks of his nickname, 'Radar Eyes,' given to him by his buddy, Henry Von Spreckelson. At night, crewmen had to dispose of ship's garbage so the debris (before it sank) could not be spotted by enemy ships in daylight hours. Huskey, accustomed to possum hunting back home, knew how to give his eyes a few minutes to adjust to the darkness before finding the hatch. Others claimed they could not find the hatch in the darkness; so they asked 'Radar Eyes' to do the job. 'Radar Eyes' could also spot a woman if there was one within five miles, his Navy buddies claimed.

These days, he has one prized reminder of the battles that affected the world: a fiftieth anniversary commemorative reunion plaque. It recognizes service in the second battle of the Phillippine Sea - the battle for Leyte Gulf, which the plaque read as the 'greatest sea battle in Naval history - October 20 through 26, 1944.'

Huskey's peaceful life by the lake is such a contrast to those battleship days named on the plaque. He and the hundreds of thousands of others, many who offered the ultimate sacrifice, lived a portion of or the final days of their lives in ways of war so foreign to us so that we might enjoy the normalcy of peaceful lives in ways we choose.

David Huskey (far left) with WWII sailor buddies.

United States Battleship Mississippi

Real Life Stories

When Ruth Fox Elder's family purchased their first radio in 1923, they were listening to KDKA Pittsburgh and to WOD Davenport, Iowa - "where the West begins," the station claimed.

Elder remembers the radio shows and typhoid fever and hearing the preaching of Billy Sunday who was once a Chicago baseball player. She has enough memories in her more-than-eighty years of living to write her own history book. Her stories, though, are better in real life because they come with a warm smile from a gracious and wise older woman who is young for her years.

The Cedar Bluff community resident was born to parents Nathanial Grant Taylor Fox and Mahalia Burchfield Fox and at the end of a large family of ten who lived to be grown. Her parents were born around Civil War times - her father, in 1865 and her mother, in 1868. One brother died in France in World War I after becoming ill with pneumonia on board a ship.

She guesses she is the fifth descendant of Adam Fox who settled here from Virginia in the late 1700's. Adam's brother, Mark, was killed by Indians and his grave is the first known Sevier County white settler grave, Elder says.

Recalling earlier times, Elder tells of hearing steam boats on the French Broad river from an upstairs room in her father's house. The sound especially carried at night or when there was a snow on the ground.

Her father's homeplace was in the bowl of English Mountain, near the Jefferson County line. He was a progressive farmer in his day, working a 200 acre farm and two smaller farms, Elder remembers. Nathanial Fox (known as Taylor or NGT) tried many new methods of farming. He worked with Sevier County's first county extension agent from the University of Tennessee... Walter O. Sharp, the one with the 'sporty little mustache,' remembers Elder.

Around 1918, farmers were trying to improve food to be shipped to European countries during World War I. They shipped much wheat overseas for the war effort while Americans were told to eat cornbread.

Elder has vivid memories of her young life. She recalls, also around 1918 or 1919, when she went to Morristown to hear Preacher Billy Sunday. a former great Chicago baseball player. The meeting was in a tobacco warehouse where folks sat on board seats that were probably over nail kegs placed around a sawdust floor. Sunday and singer/songwriter Homer Rhodehaver were greatly attended. Elder remembers the crippled preacher tell that it was better to limp into heaven than not get there at all.

A few years later, at age thirteen, Elder caught typhoid fever. Some young people were practicing for a children's program at the church and were told not to drink from a 'seepy little spring' nearby. Four little thirteen year old girls drank from the spring and all took the fever; two died.

Every day the doctor came from Jefferson County to care for young Elder. She drank small doses of iodine to kill the bacteria and to rid herself of the awful sickness and the high fever. She was too ill to eat much food, and her waist-long golden brown curls had to be cut. She took 'double infection' or a second bout with the disease which increased her dose of the iodine.

The entire large Fox family was inoculated with typhoid shots. The inoculations were so strong that they made strong men ill enough for bed for a day or so.

With the illness over, it was time for the big family to be back at work on the busy farm. Elder began having increased responsibilities at age fourteen, when her mother became ill. She recalls having cooked for big tables of hungry men. She wished she could work in Gatlinburg, but there were always too many to cook for at home. Family and farm workers were not the only folks at the Fox home; there were visitors stopping often.

At Elder's busy home of her youth, she saw a variety of folks such as once-governor Ben Hooper. She also remembers Jewish peddler Sam with his pack of lace, ribbons, and needles on his back. He was invited to stay the night, and he left behind a gift of a nice leather hand bag for Elder's mother. Sam later operated a store on Market Square in Knoxville.

Another day, she remembers a salesman carting a wood cook stove on the back of his buggy.

She talks of the first car she remembers in Fox community. It was a Reo - owned by Mr. Striplin who had the community store (near today's Forbidden Caverns.) "Striplin," she recalled, "was quite a character." If he had goods that would not sell in his store, he would have a 'throw-out', a time when he threw out the goods from an upstairs window to be taken free of charge below.

Elder's memories include places and faces that have gone. These memories are family treasures in real life stories. And that's the way it should be.

Ruth Fox Elder on her eighteenth birthday, 1928.

Mammie's Old Timey Herbs

Herb Clabo's father, 'Pap', mother, 'Mammie', he and his seven brothers and sisters lived most of Herb's growing-up years at Spruce Flats in the house farthest up the mountain in the Roaring Fork community - a part of the Great Smoky Mountains.

"Champion Fiber Company owned everything from Clingman's Dome to the Greenbrier Pinnacle. Pap (Sherman) got the use of the house and privilege of the whole territory for looking over it. He got fields to tend for corn and he pastured the woodland," said Clabo. In 1933, the family moved back to Clabo's birthplace near the end of the present day Roaring Fork Motor Nature Trail (on the same property where Clabo would later raise his own family).

Doctors and patented medicines were scarce in the Smokies when Clabo was a boy. Folks had a knowledge of mountain herbs and medicines that was essential in rearing a family when there were more illnesses and diseases than today. Clabo recalled the times when he and his brothers and sisters would dig herb roots or pull the stalk of plants for drying and sell herbs for four to five cents a pound (this, he said, compared to a working man's wages of 10 cents an hour).

"Sometimes you wouldn't sell over one bag a summer," said Clabo, with a yield of $2.50 or more for all the work.

They dug spignet (spikenard) roots for tea, solomon's seal, and cynical snake root. They picked lobelia stalk and may apples. When the herbs were dried the Clabo children packed their money-making finds on their horse, Dolly or 'Doll', and rode to a Greenbrier community store. Very little of the money the Clabo's earned was spent foolishly, said Clabo. It was mostly used for a pair of shoes or a pair of over-alls for the boys and material to make a dress for the girls. "Once in a while, we'd take a dime to go to the picture show or buy a banana to eat," said Clabo, and usually each one would buy a French harp (harmonica) or juice (jews) harp.

Every three years, the Clabos changed growing fields and grubbed new ground. While the fields sat empty, sassafras began to sprout in the spring. The scent was so pleasant, the Clabos could not resist going right out to dig the roots and make a pot of sassafras tea. Clabo said people drank the tea as a spring tonic for a blood thinner.

"Young people, back in those days, went barefooted all the time.

They got sores (the dew was poison in dog days); so, they boiled blackberry brier leaves, mixed it with lard to stay on, and put it on the sores. It was as good a medicine as you could buy," Clabo said. Clabo's mother (Beda) made burdock tea from the roots of burdock and a tea of the lady's slipper wild flower. "Mammie used to chew gensing (dried); I don't know what for," Clabo recalled, and she broke the twigs off spicewood for a spicewood tea (either for a beverage or a medicine).

Families took a dose of sulphur and molasses for a spring tonic, sort of a cure-all. They mixed a box of sulphur and a pound of lard and greased from head to toe to cure the seven year itch. The mixture was worn three or four days, the clothes washed, thrown away or buried and the person with the itch took a bath. "(The sulphur) stunk so, you couldn't put it on and go to school, 'cause everybody would know you had the itch," said Clabo. Poke root or dog hobble were used to cure the itch without the smell. Even though the seven year itch spread through schools, Clabo said you didn't want it. It was an embarrassing predicament similar to having head lice, but this itch came from under the skin, he said. And, the cure of sulphur and lard was almost as bad as the disease.

Older people in the Smokies gathered balsam sap in the Fall for heart disease and youngsters bought asafetida. It was worn at the end of a string tied around their necks, and it stank 'like all out of this world,' said Clabo. The asafetida was worn to ward off disease. "It sounds like hocus pocus, but most little kids wore it. We wore it, and we didn't have the diseases. Just like you take a flu shot and don't get (the flu). You wonder did it work or would you not have had it anyway," said Clabo.

Clabo talked as if there was no comparison in the medicine of today and when he was a boy in the Smokies. People talk about the 'good ole days,' he said. "The reason we called it good ole days is not 'cause we had to work hard to make a living or boil poke root to kill the itch. That wasn't good on nothing. It was about like killing the mange off a dog," remembered Clabo. "It was because your neighbor would come and help out when you were sick. They'd come and cook the vittles, milk the cow, strain the milk, slop the hogs, or whatever," he said. "If you were troubled about something, they would come and sit with you for hours just to talk," he said. Those are the feelings that made the ole days good, Clabo recalled.

Herb Clabo at Roaring Fork Community
Sunday afternoon singing in front of Roaring Fork School
and Church building – approximately 1924.

Fire Danger

With only Smoky Mountain black bears, the quiet, watchful bob cats, playful grey squirrels and other wild animals for company, Shirley Carver sat high on a mountain top in the Greenbrier fire tower looking out over a vast span of wilderness.

Day after day he scanned the rises and ridges of the mountains around him in search of any thread of white smoke climbing toward the skies. February through May and again from September through November, Carver made his weekly two mile hikes to the tower above the Cat Stairs at the Greenbrier Pinnacle.

From the tower, he could see all over Rich Mountain, across Chestnut Mountain and over to Cove Mountain. On clear days, he looked into Knoxville, over to Newport and out to Douglas Lake. Carver watched in the spring as the green climbed the mountains and in the fall as brilliant colors descended to lower grounds.

He lived in a ten foot by ten foot log building by the tower base with a bed, table and sink, wood stove, cistern water, and a toilet down the trail. In later years, he had a gas stove and refrigerator, hauling in two 100 pound propane tanks about twice a season in a 'motorized wheelbarrow.'

Living in this serenity and solitude, Carver sometimes was lonely for people as he watched hikers on some trail below.

Life as fire guard brought surprises. Carver remembers one morning, standing on the cabin porch drinking his coffee made with spring water. (The taste of cistern water didn't suit this country boy.) He looked up to see, a few feet away, the biggest bob cat yet — with eyes fixed on him. The visitor ended Carver's early morning coffee break on the porch.

Another time, as Carver was coming down the mountain in the snow, he was being followed by a black bear that hadn't yet denned up for winter. The bear practically chased him to his jeep as Carver picked up his pace to stay ahead of the animal.

Not all of the unexpected came on four legs; Carver tells of a group of boy scouts who visited one day. After they had gone from the tower and were out of hollering distance, Carver started to climb down. The trap door in the floor of the tower, the only way out, had been fastened from underneath by one of the boys when he placed a stick through its latch. Carver used a screw driver to remove the door and climbed down.

The fire guard probably knew every knot hole and crevice in the tiny five foot square tower shed from his many hours inside.

If conditions were right for a forest fire, if weather conditions had determined 'fire danger' or a 'four' ranking, then Carver had to remain in the tower. "If it ('fire danger') got up to eight, you didn't come out for anything," said Carver. "I have stayed in the tower up to eighteen hours," he said. Those manning the radio called Carver every thirty minutes during these high risk times.

In the tower was a round table with a stationary map of the area around Carver. When he spotted smoke, Carver called in to head-quarters his exact sighting, describing by minutes and degrees. He sighted the smoke through sights much the same as those on a gun.

Carver remembers the largest forest fire in his nine years since he began about 1962; it was on Webb's Mountain. He sat up with the fire some sixteen hours as it threatened to enter the Great Smokies. Several fires were spotted in the Cades Cove region of the Park, but Carver said most were put out before they burned out of control.

He searched his area with a powerful pair of Navy binoculars. With these, Carver said, "I could count the lug nuts on a truck on the highway."

He remembers sighting a group of boys on Norton Creek. They would set a fire, move on down the mountain and start another one. Each time one of the four or five smoke puffs came up from the ground, Carver called it in to the Sheriff's department. Deputies were waiting for the boys when they came off the mountain.

Fire threatened the Smokies more often during high wind times. Carver tells of days in the sixty-five foot tower when the wind would twist and shake the tower because there were no barriers for shield. The roaring winds would drown out the loudest of thunders. "I have been in it (the tower) when the shingles blowed off the cabin (below)," recalled Carver.

He tells, too, of how airplane pilots flew in close range. They'd come in at you, and you didn't know whether to jump or not, said Carver. He believes the fliers were army pilots using this tiny build-ing on tall legs in testing. Fliers would dive their planes by the tower as they tried to fly under radar detection, Carver said. Once a plane flew so close as Carver was descending the tower, "I was hugging the steps, not the hand rails," he said. The force took the buttons right off his shirt, he added.

Another man in another tower was sucked into the railing as he stood on the porch outside the tower when a plane flew by, the fire guard said. The way the towers were placed, it would have been many, many feet below before the guard would ever have reached solid earth - had he toppled over the rail.

Because of the seasonal nature of Carver's work, he left the tower in the early 1970's. It wasn't too many years before a helicopter came in and carried the dismantled tower off the mountain top in pieces - the same one that Civilian Conservation Corp boys had carried up the mountain in sections, said Carver.

With the towers, went a piece of another era in the history of the Great Smoky Mountains National Park.

Greenbrier Pinnacle fire tower — 1960s

God's Endowment

Mary Bond McMahan (1896 - 1983) was a teacher at one of Sevier County's three all black elementary schools before integration. She had the distinction of being the first teacher in Sevier County with a masters degree, said her great nephew and pupil Joe McMahan.

An even greater distinction in the eyes of those who knew McMahan's Aunt Mary was that of master of her trade or mentor. McMahan described the educator as impartial, a motivator, versatile, genuine... and, though childless, a mother to many of the community - black and white.

Mary McMahan, of Williamsburg, Kentucky, met her Sevier County husband - Fred McMahan while the two were attending Knoxville College. Fred McMahan, one of three brothers who owned J.F. & N. Construction, would later receive his Masters in Architectural Engineering from the University of Illinois.

In the 1920's it was J. F. & N. that donated land to build Pleasant View School where Mary McMahan taught 'across the river' (the little brick building still stands on Henderson Road in east Sevierville.) Men of the community cut the timber from the land for the building, and the brick was made and laid by black brick makers and masons whose families would attend the school. The Rosenthal Fellowship bought materials for the building and volumes for the library.

Prior to the opening of Pleasant View, students had school in New Salem Baptist Church, but McMahan said that there was often problems with flooding there.

Mary McMahan taught at Pleasant View, sometimes driven in a hack by his Aunt Florence Hodson, the school's cook. For the near forty years she taught there, there were usually about 15 students present. The numbers were few especially after World War II, because men left the county and found educational opportunities for blacks and working opportunities for their wives better elsewhere; they did not return.

McMahan attended his Aunt Mary's classes in the 1940's. He recalled her unique methods of teaching that fit the needs of all eight grades.

She taught by objectives - a term much used in education today. She delegated to older students tasks of helping the younger, he said.

She was individual in her instruction, prodding some, encouraging others, but recognizing differences and limitations, said her nephew. Education at Pleasant View was well rounded, including music and culture. "Aunt Mary was an accomplished pianist; she had a beautiful voice," said McMahan.

Day trip cultural and educational excursions were taken in Joe McMahan's school years to such places as state parks, TVA lakes, Unto These Hills drama, The Book of Job drama in Kentucky, and Oak Ridge. Motels and restaurants throughout much of this region were still not open to blacks, so Pleasant View students had to pack their lunch and return home during day trips.

Aunt Mary donated her summer time for some of the field trips and for those falling behind in their grades, and she worked in vacation Bible schools for the youth. She and others were involved in community gatherings - many of which centered around the school. McMahan recalled the fund raisers, the apple bobbings, the may poles, and picnics with Charlie Dockery's barrels of cokes cooling in ice.

He told of buying books for school from Rawlings Furniture store, and laughing, he remembered the whizzing pieces of cornbread at the school lunch table. Aunt Florence, he said, was a good cook, but her cornbread was hard; it made good weapons, but brought swift punishment.

Joe or Sonny McMahan graduated Pleasant View and said 'goodbye' to Aunt Mary's school room at age twelve. When black students graduated, before the 1960s, their education stopped in Sevier County. They either had to have relatives living in nearby counties with a larger black population or transportation to high schools in these counties. Integration was still in the future.

Driving an old pick-up truck on an under-age permit given him by then Highway Patrolman Brownlee Reagan, Joe McMahan went right on into high school at Old Austin (present day Vine, Jr.) His education by his capable Aunt prepared him for an early graduation at age sixteen.

School days under Mary McMahan's instruction laid foundation for McMahan to later receive a Masters degree from Western North Carolina University in Industrial Management... to work in personnel/labor relations at Union Carbide... and finally to operate his own Sevierville construction company.

Mary McMahan's education vaulted other students into successful professional careers. One student is an interpreter in the Swiss embassy; and one deaf mute student, she taught to talk.

The leading community role by both Mary McMahan (and her

husband — added Joe McMahan) continues to live on in east Sevierville. McMahan said, she could have walked with kings, yet through her impartiality, she maintained a common touch with those she met.

Mary Bond McMahan died in her eighties; she continued soaking up knowledge and working with her hands until then. She was a pillar in the community, firm in her faith, civic minded, and most noted of all for her love and concern for others, according to Joe McMahan. Her world of segregation did not intimidate this woman. "Your body is the temple of Christ. If you develop your God given endowment, the Lord will make a place for you," she would say.

Mrs. Mary McMahan's students at Pleasant View School,
approximately 1951.

Osie

Osie Ownby began 'frailing' a banjo when he was about five years old - more than eighty years ago. He is probably the oldest mountain musician in the Smokies. Today, he sits in a peaceful, private setting at the foot of Pine Mountain surrounded with memorabilia from years of entertaining.

Osie has chatted with Mother Maybelle Carter and Ramblin' Red Folley; he played 'Sourwood Mountain' on the Grand Ole Opry Stage and was a longtime friend of 'Grandpappy' Archie Campbell.

Born in 1909, Osie grew up on his Grandpap Levi (pronounced Leevie) Ogle and Granny Julia Ann McCarter Ogle's place at the head of Baskins Creek community. He tells of a time before his day when the early mountain people made money selling bear meat (almost as good as beef) to families down in White Oak Flats (Gatlinburg). It was before tourists, before roads, when there were only mountain trails. The men skinned the bears, he said, and hung the skins on trees to dry near Ephriam Ogle's store. The branch that ran by soon became known as Bear Skin Branch and by way of the mountain tongue translated to Baskins Creek.

The mountain banjo picker is descended from "Lyin' Tom Ogle" one of the first Ogle brothers to settle in Gatlinburg. He says the man got his nickname from his neighbors. Ogle was passing by their home when they yelled out, "Come over here and tell us a big lie."

"Lyin' Tom" replied, "Hain't got time, got to go get a doctor. Joe Huskey fell out of the barn loft and broke his arm."

The concerned neighbors went to see about Huskey only to find him out plowing his garden. "Why that 'Lyin' Tom,'" they said... then, remembered that they had jokingly said, 'come over here and tell us a big lie.' Tom just obliged his neighbors.

As his descendents before him, Osie helped on the farm. He attended church and school in the Little Valley church building at Baskins. His passtime enjoyment came from frailing the banjo. Osie's older brother bought an old time banjo at a pawn shop in Knoxville and brought it to Osie's grandfather's home. The banjo and fiddle were about the only instruments Osie heard in his younger years.

"Grandpap didn't care too much for picking and singing," remembered Osie. Rowdy musicians who were not too work brickle had given pickers a bad name in his grandfather's mind. Osie remembers waking up to breakfast one morning and seeing the remains of his brother's banjo in the fireplace. His brother had been pickin' and singin' 'ugly songs', and when the guilt became too much, he burned the banjo.

Osie learned to play that pawn shop banjo, and he learned to pick the guitar. By the 1920s, as a teenager, he picked and sang in contests at Old Timer's Day in Gatlinburg. He soon joined some buddies in a band and played as listeners filled a fruit jar with nickels and dimes and sometimes quarters. One early band included Jim Ball and Lewis Huskey, fiddlers; Henry (Shorty) Reagan who played the guitar and Osie Ownby, the banjo picker and guitar player.

Mountain folks enjoyed having a little fun, so comedy was much a part of their performances. Osie said he did not tell anything 'below the board or below the table,' and he did not care to listen to jokes of that nature.

When radio began bringing the sounds of country and bluegrass to the Great Smokies, Osie learned to yodel by listening to Jimmie Rodgers. He patted his foot to the rhythm of music by Lula Bell and Scotty, the Cumberland Ridge Runners and the Fruit Jar Drinkers. Later, this 'big eyed boy from the Smoky Mountains' talked with Bill and Charlie Monroe, and he played instruments with Grandpa Jones. He is a brother to 'Brother Oswald,' a regular on the Grand Ole Opry. and many times he has walked through the back door at the Opry for a closer look and listen to its stars.

He recalls passing by Dolly Parton at backstage as she was eating a dish of poke salad.

From his early years when Jim Ball taught him a few chords on the banjo, through the few lessons along, Osie has spent many hours picking, singing and laughing. When Earl Scruggs, Snuffy Jenkins and Shannon Grayson introduced finger style picking, Osie learned that, too.

He played on the Cas Walker show on television when folks such as Dolly Parton and Honey Wiles were performing. Bud Brewster, of the Cas Walker Show, was one excellent teacher for Osie, he recalled. The musician performed live on radio in the fifties on the Robertson Brothers and Sharp Hardware Farm and Home Hour Show in Sevierville. He worked with Jim Ball and the Mountain Boys at Homespun Valley, a Gatlinburg museum and performance show.

Once, he and some of the boys slipped a fruit jar under the drip of an authentic moonshine still at Homespun Valley. Shirley Grooms, the museum manager, worried that the jokers would get them all fired.

Osie and musician friends have enjoyed their laughs and their songs. He is a family man, too. He and wife Adis Myers Ownby have a son, James Donald, and a daughter, Mary Jane, and they have two granddaughters.

Many banjo picks have worn with use since the day Osie declared to his wife, "I'm going to learn to play the banjo, and I'm going to sell it for money!" He continues to do so, as opportunity permits, and Osie is still as enthusiastic today as one might imagine him 70 and 80 years ago with a banjo strap around his neck.

The banjo picker looks the part with his bib overalls, blue plaid shirt and bolo tie. His foot keeps time as his fingers roll and a smooth hand moves up and down the neck of the banjo. A big old mountain boy grin crosses his face and old Ose — in a clear, strong voice sings out the songs that only a mountain man can sing.

Osie Ownby, far right, with (l. to r.) Amos Trentham, Lawson Maples, Harve Reagan, and Louis Clabo — 1928 photo

Dusty Roads And A Rolling Store

Driving a rolling store down the dusty roads of Sevier County in the late 1930s was a sight that Murrell Whaley said looked like "out our way." It was a '37 or '38 model pale blue Chevrolet truck with a black wooden store attached to the bed; on the side, the words 'Butler's Rolling Store' were painted.

There was a place on top of the store for cases of eggs, over the cab was a chicken coop, and at the back was a coal oil barrel with a spigot attached.

"I'd be a goin' up, like, toward Jones Cove. I didn't know just exactly every place to stop; I looked over across the field and saw a little old boy and girl running just as hard as they could," said Whaley. He stopped and waited for the traders, probably barefoot and overall clad. "Kids usually bought candy; we sold stick candy and grocery mix. They'd bring out an egg or two in their hands to swap for the candy," he said.

And, if a mother came out and couldn't afford the candy, Whaley gave it away.

Rolling stores were in business in the thirties and forties. Whaley drove for Shirley Butler who owned Butler's Store in Pigeon Forge. Fred Atchley had four or five rolling stores and Omer Green owned others. "Not too many people had cars. People had a hard way of getting to the store," said Whaley.

He remembers Mel Large drove an old T Model Ford car in the late twenties and thirties that he used for peddling mostly vegetables. "He'd have green onions and things stuffed all over that car," he recalled.

Just inside the back opening of Butler's rolling store were scales for weighing chickens that were bartered for groceries. Shelves lined the store on either side and in front. Butler's sold coal oil for fifteen cents a gallon (many people in Sevier County were still without electricity during this period.)

A five pound bag of sugar sold for twenty-five cents, coffee (mostly JFG) sold for ten or fifteen cents a pound. There were bolts of cloth, lard, meal, flour, apples, rolling tobacco, aspirin tablets, epsom salts, Camels or Chesterfield cigarettes and salt. Bottled drinks: grape, Dr. Pepper and Coca Cola sold for a nickel each, but folks didn't buy too many soft drinks, said Whaley.

Their money was used more for the foods they had to have - like a twenty-five pound bag of Blue Bird or Red Bird flour that sold for fifty cents (and the cloth flour sack could be used to make 'sack' dresses). The rolling store carried White Lily flour, the good stuff, but it sold for about twice as much as Red Bird and Blue Bird - so it didn't sell as well.

"A three or four dollar bill of groceries was a right smart then," said Whaley, the young, single driver.

Whaley said people traded with eggs, chickens, butter, walnuts (already cracked), hams and shoulder meat. For years after trading for groceries stopped, country people would talk about going to the grocery store "to do my tradin'."

People had a way of getting the most for their trades. Whaley remembered, "This was one Saturday. It was hot that day, pretty close to 12:00, and there was a pretty big bunch of people (out to meet the peddler near Richardson's Cove).

(This lady) brought me out this big old fat hen," he said. A man stood right under the scales as Whaley placed the plump hen with its feet tied together on the scales. The hen left her own deposit right on the man's head. "It was pure bran," said Whaley. The woman had fed the hen extra bran to get more money by the pound. She was a "beat" (embarrassed) woman, but Whaley was so tickled he paid her full price anyway.

"I learned... you could tell how a woman bought stuff, whether she would 'beat' (cheat) you or not," said Whaley. If she spent on things she didn't need she was going to 'beat' you, he said. But, if she was careful with her money, she was honest. Many people bought on credit, so Whaley had to learn who would or would not pay their bill.

His six and a half (usually) eight hour days would generate about a hundred dollars each day in cash and produce. One dollar would buy a big bag of groceries, he said. The rolling store routes took Whaley into the Newport Highway/ English Mountain/Sims Chapel area, the Middlecreek/Boogertown (Oldham's Creek) area, and around Little Cove/Mill Creek/Wears Valley. He drove into Pittman Center/Webbs Creek area, to Jones Cove and in the Caney Creek/Mill Creek area.

Half way through the day Whaley would stop near a store to buy a cold soft drink and eat his 'peddler's dish' — cold pork and beans or salmon fish poured into a cut-off paper bag with crackers on the side. Sometimes, he would take along school boys who were playing 'hookie' from school.

Whaley's family had just moved to Pigeon Forge on Ore Bank Road near where he lives today in 1928, out of Greenbrier in the Smokies.

After driving the rolling store for two years he began hauling coal for "Uncle" Joe Householder, and he later married Irene Burchfield. The same as many Greenbrier Whaleys, Murrell Whaley has snowy white hair and a voice for singing. He has sung tenor in the church choir for years, and he likes a good laugh out of life.

He surely had many laughs driving the back roads of Sevier County... What a sight to see Whaley talking trade with the shrewd mountain women of the day, with one fat hog, fourteen dozen eggs, geese honking, and chickens squawking.

Murrell Whaley — late 1930s

Borrowed Overalls

Laura Elizabeth Carver Watson talks about another generation's days on a hillside farm... of riding horses, playing marbles and caring for the younger children in the family. There's more talk of climbing trees and playing baseball than there is of 'playing dolls' because Watson was too busy keeping up with older brothers.

If she had anyone to play with as a child she had to join brothers near her age because, of the ten children in her family, her sisters were born younger than she.

Watson lived her childhood years in the teens and twenties of this century in the Oldhams Creek community. Earlier, the family had lived at Greenbrier, then Smoky or Sheep Pen when she was about three. Her parents were Joseph (Jo) Allen Carver and Martha Ellen Ogle Carver from the Smokemont area of North Carolina.

She talks of early morning biscuits and gravy, of the family's milk cow Blackie, the one who kicked just about every milking time, and of the horse named Maude.

This 'tom boy' loved sports. She used hand whittled bats of perhaps hickory and a baseball made from the rolled string of an old unraveled sock. She pitched horse shoes with real shoes too worn for the horse.

It was a treat for Watson to ride with her brothers the quarter of a mile from the barn to take the family's one horse and the neighbor's two to pasture. And, said Watson, she could ride as well as the boys. It was especially fine to ride into Gatlinburg to go to the store. She enjoyed riding, but there wasn't much time for riding for sport. The horses were more for work than play.

Farming times were changing in Watson's younger years. She recalls as a very young child picking cuckleburs (cockleburs) from the wool that had been shorn from the family's sheep. Wheat was grown then, too, and threshed with Bill Whitted's threshing machine. Whitted was a neighbor from across the hill at Powder Mill. The wheat was taken to Pigeon Forge to be ground into flour; community mills were used for grinding corn.

As Watson grew older, the family began buying their flour and wool. They did, except for certain times during the Great Depression when pocketbooks were tighter.

Watson recalls wearing dresses to school made from cotton goods or cloth from the peddler Eli Wilson. Her bartered writing tablets were from the peddler, as well. The young country girl wore her one school dress to school all week, changing at the end of the school day for a pair of her brother Jason's borrowed overalls. Overalls were more fitting than a dress for swinging from grape vines and chasing after a cow.

Soon, her days of playing kick-the-can, antlie over and running base turned to days of baking egg custard pie for school pie suppers. Winfred Whaley auctioned pies that were baked by young girls and sometimes bid on by the boys who were 'sweet on' the girls. By 1935 the young Carver girl was married to Bob Watson and baking pies for her own family. Over the next twenty years the work at home that she loved so much would be made easier. First, the family purchased a gas powered washer and a gasoline or kerosene powered refrigerator, then came electricity, brighter lights, and water pumped into the home.

She thinks back today of the work and fun of childhood... the school plays, her first ride in a T Model Ford, and hearing Grand Ole Opry tunes or Chuck Wagon Gang songs on the phonograph. Those T Models and phonographs are in the past, but one part of Watson's life that remained has been her love of sports. After she quit playing basketball, horseshoes, and baseball, she became a spectator who watched her children, Lorene, Danny and Phyllis and their children on the ball fields and courts.

Old time ways shared by 'Aunt Laurie' are cherished memories to those who knew her. She has since gone on to Heaven, leaving behind rays of good will as comforting as the morning sun. 'Aunt Laurie' lived a good life; she had a quiet spoken voice offering kind words for others. The 'virtuous woman' in Proverbs was descriptive of Laura Elizabeth Carver Watson.

Hard Work And A Kind Heart

He rises before daylight, pulls on a pair of high back overalls and laces up the heavy brogan shoes on his feet. He pours warm water from off the wood cook stove into the wash pan, and he dips his shaving brush into a mug of lather. In front of the looking glass, Pa carefully scrapes the three day beard from his face with his straight razor.

Before breakfast, Pa takes his gun down from the wall, places a few shells in his pocket, and reaches for his cap and jacket from the nail on the back of the door.

The squirrels have been cutting hickory nuts over in the new ground, and Pa has decided to bring two or three home for supper. He walks over creek rocks and climbs the steep hillside with only a hint of morning light to light his way.

Pa sits by the trunk of a big oak and listens to the birds tweetering and chirping. As the sun tops the trees, he can see little patches of mist hanging on spider webs, and he looks off in the distance to the next ridgetop, contemplating where he'll cut the winter firewood.

Back at home, he sits down to a plate running over with gravy and biscuits and side meat. He tells the boys to go and hitch the mule to the sled so they can haul in yesterday's cutting of wood.

With a crosscut saw over his shoulder and the boys bringing along the axe and wedge and a bucket of drinking water, Pa has his morning work ahead.

The saw's teeth cut quickly through the tree, because Pa and his son have done this job many times before. The two work in rhythm as they push and pull the blade at a fast pace.

After 'ballhooting' the pieces of wood down the hill, it is loaded on the sled. The family mule stops munching grass and pulls the sled to the woodshed.

Pa and the others fill up on corn bread and beans at the dinner table. They move out to the porch where he leans back in the straight chair and pulls out a whittling knife.

By the end of the day, Pa and his family have added to the wood pile for the cookstove and for the winter. They have much more corn out of the field to be shucked and shelled for taking to the mill and for chicken and animal feed.

After supper, Pa takes the time to show his children how to make a whistle from a pumpkin stalk, and then they sit outside on this cool late-summer evening to talk and look at the stars.

Before he and Ma lie down for sleep, he will kneel by his bed in thanks. Only the night before, Pa was out riding through the darkness for the doctor to help his young one survive until daybreak. He is thankful for the Lord's guiding hand in sickness and His comfort to worried parents.

Let our prayers of today include giving thanks for all the hardworking fathers with a kind heart.

INDEX